MW00789575

# THE SUCCESS
# SUTRA

Also by Devdutt Pattanaik

*Business Sutra: A Very Indian Approach to Management*

*Jaya: An Illustrated Retelling of the Mahabharata*

*Sita: An Illustrated Retelling of the Ramayana*

*Myth=Mithya: A Handbook of Hindu Mythology*

*Pashu: Animal Tales from Hindu Mythology*

*Shikhandi: And Other Tales They Don't Tell You*

*The Pregnant King: A Novel*

*Shiva to Shankara: Decoding the Phallic Symbol*

*The Goddess in India: The Five Faces of the Eternal Feminine*

# THE SUCCESS
# SUTRA

## AN INDIAN APPROACH TO WEALTH

# DEVDUTT
# PATTANAIK

*Illustrated by the author*

ALEPH

ALEPH

ALEPH BOOK COMPANY
An independent publishing firm
promoted by *Rupa Publications India*

Published in India in 2015 by
Aleph Book Company
7/16 Ansari Road, Daryaganj
New Delhi 110 002

ISBN: 978-93-84067-41-0

5 7 9 10 8 6 4

Printed and bound in India by
Thomson Press India Ltd, Faridabad

# Contents

# Introduction

There was once a priest who was very poor, there were constant quarrels in his house between his unhappy wife, his hungry children and his helpless parents. He begged the deity of his temple to help. So the deity gave him a pot of gold. The happy priest sold the gold and used the money to repay his debts, bought all the things money could buy, and even made investments to secure his future. But soon after the quarrels started again: between his greedy wife, his ambitious children and his neglected parents. Each one wanted a greater share of the treasure. Annoyed, the priest went to the deity and demanded a solution. Once again the deity gave him a pot of gold. "No, I don't want another pot of gold. Give me something that solves the problem truly," cried the priest. "Pot of gold!" exclaimed the deity, "but I never gave you a pot of gold. I gave you the nectar of wisdom. Did you not drink it? Or were you too distracted by the container?"

This story illustrates Indian beliefs about wealth and success. Within every fortune (the pot of gold) lies wisdom, an idea to be trusted: a belief that makes success sustainable. These beliefs play a key role in business and management. They determine choices and catalyse the decisions of buyers and sellers, regulators and shareholders, investors and entrepreneurs, employers and employees, vendors and customers. They determine how we do business. This book shows how Indian beliefs, transmitted through ancient stories (also pots of gold), may be used to create a unique approach to success in business and life in general.

Ancient Indians saw business as yagna, the ritual described in the oldest and most revered of Hindu scriptures, the Rig Veda.

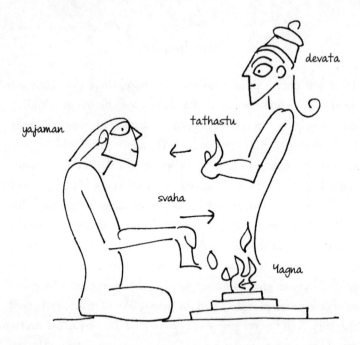

The yajaman initiates this ritual, makes offerings into agni, the fire burning in the altar, exclaiming "svaha"—this of me I offer, hoping to please his chosen deity or devata who will then give him whatever he desires, exclaiming "tathastu"—so it shall be. Svaha is what the yajaman invests: goods, services and ideas. Tathastu is the return on investment: revenue in the marketplace or salary paid by the employer, or even the services offered by the employee. It all depends on who plays the role of the yajaman, who initiates the yagna. The yagna can operate both downstream, as well as upstream, so the devata can either be the buyer or the seller, the investor or the entrepreneur, the employer or employee, director or doorman.

Business is about generating Lakshmi, the goddess of wealth in Hinduism as well as in Buddhism and Jainism. Conventionally, business starts by articulating the tathastu (target) first, then the plan and resources for executing the svaha (tasks). Skills come later. What matters are the offering, the gestures and the exclamations; in other words, the process. The personality of the yajaman does not matter. His fears do not matter. His feelings do not matter. In fact, he is expected to be a professional, act without emotion. Besides, he is always replaceable, making the yagna more important than the yajaman.

But, according to Vedic scriptures, the yagna had no independent existence outside the yajaman. Business is always about people: of people, by people, for people. Everything hinges on the bhaav of the yajaman towards the devata, the feeling with which he offers the svaha and receives the tathastu. Bhaav also means value. The feeling of the yajaman determines the value he grants to the devata.

The more dependable a yajaman is, the more he is able to attract the devatas, as bees to nectar. The devatas in turn will churn out Lakshmi for him from the ocean of milk that is the marketplace.

Every interaction in business is a yagna, be it between investor and entrepreneur, employer and employee, manager and executive, professional and vendor, seller and buyer. The yagna is the fundamental unit of business, where everything that can satisfy hunger is exchanged. Animals cannot exchange (though some trading and accounting behaviours have been seen in a few species of bats). Exchange is a human innovation that reduces the effort of finding food. It increases the chances of getting fed. It improves the variety of food we get access to. Exchange creates the marketplace, the workplace, even the family. It is the cornerstone of society.

Svaha is food for the devata. Tathastu is food for the yajaman. Unless svaha is given, tathastu cannot be expected. As is svaha, so is tathastu. Ideally, the yajaman wants the devata to give tathastu voluntarily, joyfully, responsibly and unconditionally. When this happens, it is said Lakshmi walks his way.

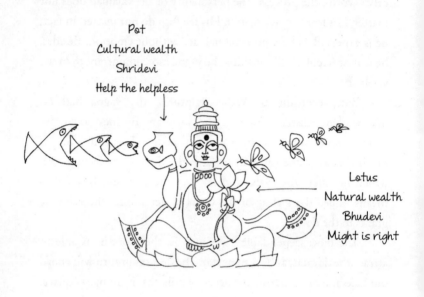

Pot
Cultural wealth
Shridevi
Help the helpless

Lotus
Natural wealth
Bhudevi
Might is right

Today, everywhere we look, there are actions that have resulted in the absence of Lakshmi (poverty), as jungle law (might is right) is favoured over cultural norms (help the helpless). Many valorize Lakshmi's rejection through monasticism, and with derisive words like 'bazaaru' and 'dhanda' we equate professionalism and commerce with prostitution. These actions individually and collectively amount to Lakshmi-ninda, or the abuse of wealth. Time then to do Lakshmi-shruti, a re-appreciation of the goddess who nourishes life. Only then will the legendary golden bird of prosperity (sone ki chidiya) return to this rose-apple continent we call India.

*The Success Sutra*, a work derived from my book on the Indian approach to business and management, *Business Sutra*, focuses on sutras related to decision-making, the inherent violence of production, the seduction while selling and the churning of the market through forces and counterforces within organizations.

Ideas in this book are provided in the form of 'sutras'. Sutra (the word or concept) has two meanings:

- It means a string that joins dots to create a pattern. The book strings together myriad ideas from Jain, Hindu and Buddhist traditions to create a synthesized whole, that helps us understand the Indian way. Likewise it strings together Greek and biblical ideas to understand the Western way and Confucian and Taoist ideas to understand the Chinese way. Each one of these garlands is man-made and reveals my truth, not the truth.

- Sutra also means an aphorism, a terse statement. The book is full of these. They are like seeds which, when planted in the mind, germinate into plants. The nature of the plant will depend on the quality of the mind. Indian sages avoided the written word as they realized ideas were never definitive; they were transformed depending on the intellectual and emotional abilities of the giver as well as the receiver. Thus an idea is organic. Many sages chose symbols rather than sutras to communicate the idea. What appears like a naked man to one person, will reveal the nature of the mind to another. Both are right from their point of view. There is no standard answer. There is no correct answer. The point is to keep expanding the mind to accommodate more views and string them into a single whole.

These sutras are 'made in India' but are 'for the world', for they complement modern management by drawing attention back from profit, through hunger, to humanity.

# THE SUCCESS SUTRA

*Decisions*        *Violence*        *Seduction*        *Churning*

The ability to see the human quest for wealth is drishti. Plants grow seeking sunlight and water. Animals run seeking pastures and prey. The fear of starvation makes food the ultimate target or 'laksh'. From laksh comes Lakshmi, the goddess of food, the embodiment of bhog or consumption. Lakshmi is the most primal of hungers; she sustains the physical body, or sthula-sharira.

It is the fear of starvation and the quest for food that makes animals mark territories and organize themselves into pecking orders where the strongest animal in the pack, the alpha, dominates and so gets the most food, increasing his chances of survival, while the weakest, the omega, survives on the leftovers, often turning into food for another predator. It is hunger that makes animals compete.

Humans reject the way of the jungle. Imagination allows Brahma to seek maximum food even if he is weak and powerless. From imagination comes the vision of a world where the helpless are helped and even the unfit can thrive. And so he creates the pot.

While animals have to go to a water body to quench their thirst, humans can drink water whenever and wherever they wish, and give it to whomever they want, thanks to the pot. The pot represents the human capability to innovate. It enables humanity to break free from the constraints of nature.

Lakshmi holds a lotus in one hand and a pot in the other. The lotus represents natural wealth or Bhudevi while the pot represents cultural wealth or Shridevi. The nectar of the lotus is available to whichever bee gets to it first. The contents of the pot, however, are available only to the owner of the pot and to whomsoever the pot is

3

bequeathed. This can never happen in nature. This can only happen in sanskriti, which means society, but can also mean culture (which is the sense in which I have used it in this book).

In Jain mythology, a yajaman who makes pots to convert Bhudevi to Shridevi walks the path of the vasudev, which literally translates to mean 'master of the earth and the elements'. Vasudev is shalaka-purush, a worthy being, an action-driven hero who fights on behalf of his pacifist brother—the baladev—a victim of the prati-vasudev, or the villain.

- Vasudev takes decisions and makes things happen, taking full responsibility for the consequences.
- He knows that without violence the wealth of the earth cannot be drawn out.
- He knows that things need not be done nastily; there is always a nice way to do things.
- He knows how to churn, pull and push, adapt, transform the rigid organization into a nimble organism.

In this book, we shall explore decisions, violence, seduction and churning and by doing so appreciate the vasudev's gaze. A yajaman who possesses drishti and seeks Lakshmi, walks the path of the vasudev. A vasudev's gaze is that of the passionate entrepreneur who appreciates the elusive nature of wealth.

---

Mandeep can see an opportunity. The new bus stop will attract a lot of people. And people need tea and snacks. Opening a tea stall next to the bus stop will allow him to be independent. He has slaved at a tea stall in the station for years and knows what it takes to run such an enterprise. All he needs is some money and the support of local authorities. He will need to charm a few people for capital, seek favours from others and force his way to realize his dream. His boss will not be supportive but if he gets the backing of the local don, no one can stop him. The police may harass him, but even they need tea. Mandeep is a vasudev, unafraid of a fight, determined to create the pot that will harness Lakshmi.

---

*Decisions*

Key to the yagna is the decision: the willingness to pour svaha into the fire. Once poured, it cannot be pulled back. Not everyone takes decisions. Few want to be responsible for the escalating cost and the unpredictable consequences of an investment. Humans are the only living creatures who can, and do, outsource decision-making.

# He who takes a call is a karta

In the epic Ramayan, Sita finds herself in a predicament. She is alone in the middle of the forest. Her husband, Ram, and brother-in-law, Lakshman, are away on a hunt. A line has been drawn around her hut. She has been told very clearly that only within the line do the laws of culture apply; here she is Ram's wife. Outside is nature, where the rules of marriage make no sense; she is just a woman for the taking.

A hermit standing outside the line asks for some food. She invites him in but he refuses explaining that as she is alone it would be inappropriate for him to enter. She stretches her hand over the line and offers him food. This annoys the hermit. He demands she step outside and feed him properly.

Must she or must she not? If she does step out, she brings her family honour by being a good host, but she takes a huge risk as she makes herself vulnerable. If she does not, she protects herself but condemns a hermit to hunger. What matters more: hospitality or security?

Sita steps out.

Had she obeyed her husband without any thought, she would have been the karya-karta, or the obedient follower, and he the karta, or the responsible leader. But the instructions were given to her in a context very different from the one she encountered; there was no hungry hermit then. Now a hungry hermit stood outside the hut; would Ram have allowed a hermit to starve to secure his wife?

Sita chooses to take a call. She is not obliged to, yet she takes the responsibility upon herself. That proactivity transforms her into a karta, a doer, regardless of the fact that her decision did not

9

serve her well. The hermit turns out to be the rakshasa-king, Ravan, who abducts her.

To build a business, we need decision-makers and decision-followers. He who takes decisions is the karta. He who follows decisions is called a karya-karta.

After the interview, Mahmood asks Rajiv, the head of his human resource department, to stay back. They are about to select the Chief Operating Officer for the telecom division of the business. Mahmood is anxious. It is a huge risk, hiring a foreigner with no experience of India. To retain him, they have to assure him a golden parachute: compensation should the company terminate the contract before the stipulated three years. But Hugh, who has been selected, has knowledge the company desperately needs. "Will it work?" Mahmood asks. Rajiv keeps quiet. There are no guarantees. Only time will tell. Ultimately, the boss has to decide. Rajiv will diligently obey. Mahmood is the karta and Rajiv is the karya-karta.

# Everyone is a potential karta

The mind of every human being can be compared to the mythic serpent Adi-Ananta-Sesha whose name translated literally means One-Infinity-Zero. Narayan sleeps in the coils of this serpent. Vishnu sits on it. Sesha, the coiled hoodless state, is like a dormant mind that does not think or take a decision. Ananta, the state with infinite unfurled hoods, is like a mind full of ideas. Adi, the state with a single hood, is like a focused mind, ready to strike; this is the mind of the karta.

Animals take decisions all the time. Only humans have the option not to take decisions. We can outsource decision-making to the karta and stay a karya-karta. We may even choose not to follow the decisions of a karta, like an impudent devata who needs to be cajoled or forced into action. When we choose to help others take decisions, we transform into yajamans. A yajaman is a karta too; but all kartas are not yajamans.

Thus humans have a choice to be proactive like a decision-making karta or a decision-enabling yajaman. We also have a choice to be reactive like a decision-following karya-karta or a reluctant devata.

We can let the serpent of the mind stay coiled or spring out its many hoods. Only we can make it strike.

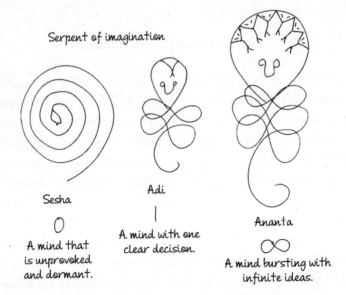

Serpent of imagination

**Sesha**

O

A mind that is unprovoked and dormant.

**Adi**

|

A mind with one clear decision.

**Ananta**

∞

A mind bursting with infinite ideas.

---

When the customer walks into the shop and Babulal does not engage with him, it is the Sesha state of slumber when no exchange take place. When the customer makes a request and Babulal reacts immediately; thus does Sesha turn into Adi. Babulal can return to the Sesha state or stir Ananta in the customer by a simple question, "Anything else you wish to buy?" This one question provokes thoughts and ideas in the customer's mind, infinite ideas are unfurled, and there is a possibility of more business.

---

*Devdutt Pattanaik*

## A karta who allows and enables others to take a call is a yajaman

One day, the sage Narad asks Vishnu, with a bit of hesitation, "Why do you insist that the image of Garud be placed before you in your temples? Why not me? Am I not your greatest devotee?"

Before Vishnu can reply a crash is heard outside the main gate of Vaikuntha. "What was that?" asks Vishnu. Garud, Vishnu's eagle and vehicle, who usually investigates such events, is nowhere to be seen. "I have sent Garud on an errand. Can you find out what happened, Narad?" asks Vishnu. Eager to please Vishnu, Narad runs out to investigate. "A milkmaid tripped and fell," he says when he returns.

"What was her name?" asks Vishnu. Narad runs out, speaks to the maid and returns with the answer, "Sharda."

"Where was she going?" asks Vishnu. Narad runs out once again, speaks to the maid and returns with the answer, "She was on her way to the market."

"What caused her to trip?" asks Vishnu. "Why did you not ask this question the last time I went?" mumbles Narad irritably. He then runs out, speaks to the maid once again. "She was startled by a serpent that crossed her path," he says on his return. "Anything else?" he asks.

"Are all her pots broken?" asks Vishnu. "I don't know," snaps Narad. "Find out," insists Vishnu. "Why?" asks Narad. "Find out, Narad. Maybe I would like to buy some milk," says Vishnu patiently. With great reluctance, Narad steps out of Vaikuntha and meets the milkmaid. He returns looking rather pleased, "She broke one pot. But there is another one intact. And she is willing to sell the milk

13

but at double price."

"So how much should I pay her?" asks Vishnu. "Oh, I forgot to ask. I am so sorry," says Narad running out once again. "Do not bother. Let me send someone else," says Vishnu.

Just then, Garud flies in. He has no idea of what has transpired between Vishnu and Narad. Vishnu tells Garud, "I heard a crashing sound outside the main gate. Can you find out what happened?" As Garud leaves, Vishnu whispers, "Let us see how he fares."

Garud returns and says, "It is a milkmaid called Sharda. She was on her way to the market. On the way, a snake crossed her path. Startled she fell down and broke one of the two pots of milk she was carrying. Now she wonders how she will make enough money to pay for the broken pot and the spilt milk. I suggested she sell the milk to you. After all, you are married to Lakshmi, the goddess of wealth."

"And the price of the milk?" asks Vishnu. Pat comes Garud's reply, "Four copper coins. One actually but I think she hopes to make a handsome profit when dealing with God." Vishnu starts to laugh. Garud always anticipates situations and takes calls accordingly without checking with his boss or master. In that micro-context, he behaves as karta.

Vishnu's eye caught Narad's and Narad understood in that instant why Garud's statue, and not his was always placed before the image of Vishnu in Vishnu temples.

Despite being given the freedom to take decisions, Narad chooses to stay karya-karta, follow decisions rather than take them, as he is too afraid of the consequences. Garud, on the other hand, anticipates the needs of Vishnu, decides to enquire voluntarily and is thus a karta. Vishnu who allows Garud to be a karta is a yajaman.

Arindam realizes the value of Meena as a team member over Ralph. Both are good workers. But when Arindam has to go for a meeting with Meena, she gives him a file with all relevant details about the client so that he can prepare well. Ralph will do no such thing. When Arindam points this out, Ralph says, "Is that the process? Do you want me to do that? I will do that, no problem." Arindam realizes that Ralph is no Garud.

# A yajaman has the power to take and give life

The sage Vishwamitra storms into the kingdom of Ayodhya and demands that the crown prince Ram accompany him to the forest and defend his hermitage from rakshasas. King Dashrath offers his army instead, as he feels Ram is too young, but Vishwamitra insists on taking Ram. With great reluctance, Dashrath lets Ram go.

In the forest, Vishwamitra points to Tataka, the female leader of the rakshasas, and asks that she be killed. When Ram hesitates because he has been taught never to raise his hand against a woman, Vishwamitra argues that a criminal has no gender. Ram accordingly raises his bow and shoots Tataka dead.

Later, Vishwamitra shows Ram a stone that was once Ahalya, the wife of Gautama, cursed to become so after her husband caught her in an intimate embrace with Indra. Vishwamitra asks Ram to step on the stone and liberate the adulteress. When Ram hesitates because he has been taught the rules of marriage should always be respected, Vishwamitra argues that forgiveness is as much a part of marriage as fidelity. Ram accordingly places his feet on the stone and sets Ahalya free from her curse.

Ram, well-versed in theory, is thus given practical lessons about being a yajaman: he will be asked to take life as well as give life. At times, he will be expected to be ruthless. At other times, he will be expected to be kind.

In business, the yajaman has the power to give a person a livelihood, grant him a promotion, sideline him or even fire him. These decisions have a huge impact on the lives of the devatas who depend on the business.

Who do I save?
Who do I kill?
What is right?
What are the consequences?

---

One day, Jake is asked by his boss to fire an incompetent employee. While the reasons are justified, Jake finds it the toughest thing to do. He has several nights of anxiety before he can actually do it. Then, a few weeks later, Jake is asked to mentor a junior employee who has been rejected by the head of another department. This is even tougher as the junior employee is rude and lazy and impossible to work with. Jake struggles and finally succeeds in getting work done through the junior employee. Jake does not realize it but his boss is being a Vishwamitra mentoring a future king.

---

## The size of the contribution does not matter

To rescue Sita, Ram raises an army of animals and gets them to build a bridge across the sea to the island-kingdom of Lanka where Sita is being held captive by the rakshasa-king Ravan.

Vultures survey the location. Bears serve as the architects. Monkeys work on implementing the construction, carrying huge boulders and throwing them into the sea. The work is tedious. The monkeys are jumping and screeching everywhere to ensure everything is being done efficiently and effectively. Suddenly, there appears amongst them a tiny squirrel carrying a pebble.

This little creature also wants to contribute to the bridge-building exercise. The monkeys who see him laugh. One even shoves the squirrel aside considering him an over-enthusiastic nuisance.

But when Ram glances at the squirrel, he is overwhelmed with gratitude. He thanks the tiny creature for his immense contribution. He brushes his fingers over the squirrel's back to comfort him, giving rise to the stripes that can be seen even today, a sign of Ram's acknowledgement of his contribution.

In terms of proportion, the squirrel's contribution to the bridge is insignificant. But it is the squirrel's 100 per cent. The squirrel is under no obligation to help Ram, but he does, proactively, responsibly, expecting nothing in return. Ram values the squirrel not for his percentage of contribution to the overall project but because he recognizes a yajaman. A squirrel today, can be a Ram tomorrow.

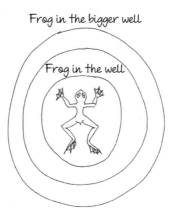

Frog in the bigger well

Frog in the well

Proportions or matra play a key role in Indian philosophy. The scale of a problem has nothing to with the potential of the decision-maker. A kupa-manduka, or frog in a well, and a chakravarti, or emperor of the world, are no different from each other, except in terms of scale. Both their visions are limited by the frontier of the land they live in. In case of the frog, it is the wall of the well. In case of the king, it is the borders of his kingdom. Both can be, in their respective contexts, generous or prejudiced. To expand scale, both have to rise.

---

Whenever Mr. Lal goes to his factory, he makes sure he speaks to people at all levels, from workers to supervisors to managers to accountants to security people. He is not interested in finding out who did the job well or who did not. That, he feels, is the job of managers. He is only interested in identifying people in the factory who take proactive steps to solve a problem. He consciously seeks decision-makers, like the executive who prepared a report on waste management without being asked to, or the supervisor who voluntarily motivated his team to clean the toilets when the housekeeping staff went on strike. For Mr. Lal these 'squirrels' who take responsibility are talents to be nurtured.

---

# All calls are subjective

The *Kathasaritsagar* tells the story of a sorcerer who requests Vikramaditya, king of Ujjain, to fetch him a vetal or ghost that hangs upside down like a bat from a tree standing in the middle of a crematorium. "Make sure you do not talk to the vetal; if you speak, he will slip away from your grasp," warns the sorcerer.

Vikramaditya enters the crematorium, finds the tree, and the vetal hanging upside down from its branches. He catches the ghost, pulls it down and begins to make his way back to the city when the ghost starts chatting with him, telling him all kinds of things, annoying him, yelling into his ears, cursing him, praising him, anything to make him speak but Vikramaditya refuses to succumb to these tricks.

Finally, the vetal tells Vikramaditya a story (a case study?), and at the end of it asks the king a question. "If you answer this question, then you are indeed Vikramaditya, a king, a yajaman who thinks and takes decisions. But if you stay quiet, and simply follow orders, you are no Vikramaditya. You are a pretender, a mere karya-karta, who simply follows orders."

Vikramaditya cannot bear being called a pretender or a karya-karta. So he speaks and answers the question with a brilliant answer. The vetal gasps in admiration.

However, almost immediately after that the wily ghost slips away, cackling without pause and goes back to hanging upside down from the tree in the crematorium.

The next night, Vikramaditya walks back to the tree and once again pulls the vetal down. The vetal tells him another story with a question at the end. Once again the vetal tells the king, "If you are indeed the wise Vikramaditya, as you claim to be, you should be able to judge this case. So answer my question. And if you choose to stay silent, I am free to assume I have been caught by a commoner, a pretender, a mimic!" Once again the proud king gives the answer to which the vetal gasps in admiration. And once again he slips away with a cackle.

This happens twenty-four times. The twenty-fifth time, a tired and exasperated Vikramaditya sighs in relief. He has succeeded.

"Have you really?" asks the vetal. "How do you know the answers you gave the previous times were right? All answers are right or wrong only in hindsight. You made decisions because you thought they were right. The answer would have been subjective this time, too. Only now, you are not sure of the answer, you hesitate, and so remain silent. This silence will cost you dear. You will succeed in taking me to the sorcerer who will use his magic to make me his genie and do his bidding. His first order for me will be to kill you. So you see, Vikramaditya, as long as you were karta, taking calls, you were doing yourself a favour. As soon as you stop making your own decisions, stop being a karta, you are at the mercy of others and you are sure to end up dead."

Everyone looks at the karta for a decision despite data being unreliable, the future being uncertain, and outcomes that are unpredictable. Not everyone can do it. He who is able to make decisions independently is the karta. He who allows others to do so is the yajaman.

---

The investors are chasing Deepak. He built an online coaching class of engineering students that was bought by a large educational portal for a phenomenal amount. Now the investors expect Deepak to repeat this success. Deepak is filled with self-doubt. He is not sure what it was about the website he built that made it so valuable in the eyes of the buyers. Was it just luck? Since he does not know what made him successful, how can he repeat the success? There was nothing objective about his creation. Must he follow his gut instincts again? But the investors will not allow him to do so; their auditors will keep asking him for explanations and reasons, assuming his calls are rational. And the media, which celebrated the sale, is watching his every move continuously. He is a victim of success. How he wishes he never became an entrepreneur. How he wishes he could roll back the clock, be a simple engineer working in a factory, diligently doing what the boss tells him to do.

---

# All decisions are contextual

Amongst the twenty-five stories that the vetal told Vikramaditya, this is one: a king killed a merchant and laid claim to all his property. The merchant's widow fled the kingdom swearing revenge. She seduced a priest and was impregnated by him. She abandoned the son thus born at the door of a childless king who adopted the foundling and raised him as his own. "Who is the father of this child: the merchant who was married to his mother, the priest who made his mother pregnant or the king who adopted him?"

Vikramaditya replies with the caveat that the answer would depend on the culture to which the king belongs. In some cultures only biological fathers matter, in some, legal fathers matter and in others, foster fathers matter more. There is no objective answer in matters related to humans.

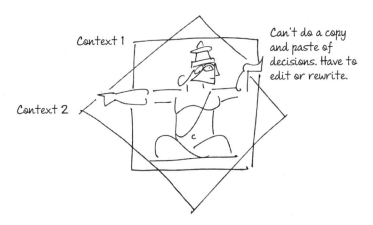

In the Mahabharat, Pandu is called the father of the Pandavs even though he is not their biological father. The law of the land states that a man is the father of his wife's children. The Pandavs demand a share of Pandu's kingdom on the basis of this law. Is this law the right law? At Kurukshetra, the Pandavs kill Bhisma, the man who raised them as a foster father would, because he fights on the opposing side. Is that ethical? In the Ramayan, Ram is celebrated for being faithful to one wife, yet in the Mahabharat, men have many wives and the Pandavs even share a common wife. What is appropriate conduct?

Laws by their very nature are arbitrary and depend on context. What one community considers fair, another may not consider to be fair. What is considered fair by one generation is not considered fair by the next. Rules always change in times of war and in times of peace, as they do in times of fortune and misfortune.

Thus, no decision is right or wrong. Decisions can be beneficial or harmful, in the short-term or long-term, to oneself or to others. Essentially, every decision has a consequence, no matter which rule is upheld and which one is ignored. This law of consequence is known as karma.

---

Mr. Gupta has to choose a successor. Should it be his eldest son who is not very shrewd? Should it be the second son who is smart but not interested in the business? Must it be his daughter, who feels gender should not be a criterion, but who fails to realize she is not really that smart? Should it be his brilliant son-in-law, who does not belong to the community, which will annoy a lot of shareholders? Must the decision be based on emotion, equality, fairness, loyalty, or the growth of the business and shareholder value? Each and every answer will have opponents. Must he simply divide the business before he dies for the sake of peace or let his two sons and daughter fight it out in court after his death? There is no right answer, he realizes. Traditionally, in the community, the eldest son inherited everything. That was convenient but often disastrous. Mr. Gupta does not want to impress the community; he wants his legacy to outlive him. He also wants all his children to be happy. His desires impact the decision as much as the context.

_____

# Not everyone can handle the burden of uncertainty

One day, Bhartrihari receives a jewel from a traveller who is visiting his kingdom. "Only a king such as you is worthy of possessing it," says the traveller.

That night, the king gives the jewel to his beloved queen because he feels she is more worthy of it.

The next day, to his great surprise, he finds the same jewel in a basket full of dung being carried by the lady who cleans the stables.

On being questioned, the cleaning lady says it has been given to her by her lover, the man who grooms the royal horses. When the groom is accused of theft, he reveals it is a gift from a nymph who visits him every night in the stables. The king decides to investigate.

The following night, Bhartrihari hides in the stables and realizes that the 'nymph' is none other than his beloved queen! Blinded by love, he does not see that his wife loves another man and she does not see that the man she finds attractive cares for another woman.

After this incident, the king is unable to take any decisions. He doubts everything he sees. Uncertainty paralyzes him. He trusts no one. In despair, he decides to become a hermit and give up his throne to his younger brother, Vikramaditya.

Bhartrihari has to confront the horror of human existence. We can never know everything and we can never be sure. All information is incomplete, and all readings distorted by personal prejudice. And yet we have to take decisions all the time and hope the results favour us. Bhartrihari feels powerless. He is unable to conduct the yagna and passes on the reins of his kingdom to his younger brother, Vikramaditya.

While everyone has the potential of being a karta or a yajaman, not everyone is willing to take decisions and be responsible for the outcome. We would rather be devata (reactive) than yajaman (proactive).

---

Madhukar, head of marketing, recommends that Arshiya be made the head of corporate communications. Soon after her promotion, Arshiya begins to behave very differently. She becomes more arrogant and imperious. She is no longer as gentle or as kind. Madhukar realizes that as long as Arshiya reported to him, she behaved very nicely. Now that she reports directly to the managing director, she is not obliged to be nice. Madhukar realizes that the data on the basis of which he made the recommendation was false. He decides to never again recommend anyone for a job or promotion. Ergo, he will never be a yajaman again.

---

Does she really love me?

Does she pretend to love me?

Does she love her idea of me?

Does he love what I have?

# Every decision has a consequence

In the Ramayan, Dashrath shoots an arrow in the direction of a sound that he believes to be the sound of deer drinking water. It turns out to be the sound of water being collected in a pot. The arrow fatally injures the young man who was fetching the water. The young man is Shravan. His old and blind parents do not see this event as an accident. They see it as murder. They curse Dashrath to, like them, die of heartbreak following separation from his son.

In the Mahabharat, Pandu shoots an arrow at a deer, not realizing that it is copulating with a doe, and that it is, in fact, no deer but a sage called Kindama who has taken the form of a deer, along with his wife, in order to mate in the open air. Kindama curses Pandu that should he touch a woman and try to have sex with her, he will die instantly. As a result, Pandu cannot father children. He feels he is unfit to be king as he will never father an heir. So he renounces the throne and stays in the jungle, choosing to be a hermit, a decision that takes everyone in the palace by surprise.

The notion of karma is unique to Indian thought. No action exists in isolation. Every decision impacts the ecosystem. Karma is often mistaken for the adage, "As you sow, so shall you reap." The assumption then is that if we sow good deeds, we will reap good rewards. But who decides what action is good or bad? The desire to qualify an action, and its consequence, as good or bad, right or wrong, is a peculiarly human trait. Nature does not do so.

Action impacts the self, the people around and the environment at large. Every person is impacted at three levels: the physical level, the mental level and the social level. Thus, a tiny ripple can result in a storm, and the ripple-causer needs to take responsibility for it.

An arrow that has been released from the bow is a metaphor for a decision that cannot be withdrawn. It has consequences that a yajaman has to face. There is no escape. This is a heavy burden to bear.

Because you became rich, I appear poor. Because you succeeded, I am now expected to succeed too. You make me feel inadequate. I hate you. I envy you.

I don't deserve this. I just wanted to be rich.

For years, they manufactured automobile parts. But when Ritwik decides they should open service centres for luxury cars, the whole family opposes him. "Do it with your own money!" his brother says. So Ritwik uses his own money and investments. If he succeeds, the profits are his alone. He will prove once and for all that he is smarter than the rest of his family. If he fails, he will have to face the double humiliation of being a business failure and being told by his family, "We told you so." If Ritwik chooses to listen to his family, he will have to spend the rest of his life wondering about all the things that could have happened if only he had had the guts to take a risk. There is no escape from consequences.

# Decisions are good or bad only in hindsight

Garud, the eagle, is enjoying the song of a sparrow atop Mount Kailas when he observes Yama, the god of death, also looking at the bird. But Yama is frowning. Maybe he does not like the song. Fearing for the welfare of the little bird, Garud, with compassion in his heart, decides to take the bird away from Yama's line of sight.

Garud takes the bird in the palm of his hand and flies to a forest far away, beyond the seven mountains and seven rivers. There, he leaves the sparrow on a tree full of succulent fruits. When he returns to Mount Kailas, he finds Yama smiling. Yama explains, "My account books are balanced. I saw a sparrow here singing a song. It was supposed to die today but not here. It was supposed to die in a forest far beyond the seven mountains and seven rivers, eaten by a python that lives under a tree full of succulent fruits. This has happened, thanks to you, Garud."

Garud realizes in hindsight that what he thought was an act of kindness turned out to be an act of cruelty for the sparrow.

When strategies are made it is in the hope that they will minimize surprises. Huge amounts of time are taken to ensure the data and the analysis is right so that the results are predictable. As organizations grow larger, the cost of mistakes is higher, and so much more time and energy is taken while taking decisions. And yet, despite all precautions, things can and do go wrong, often because assumptions are incorrect. A yajaman needs to take this in his stride.

A yajaman needs to be defined not by the outcome, achievement, goal or performance, but by his ability to take decisions proactively and responsibly.

It seemed like the right thing to do at the time: leaving the job and starting out on his own. Parul thought that the clients would love to have the same work done at a lower cost by a freelance consultant. But when she started visiting clients she realized there were more freelance consultants than she had anticipated. The competition was fierce. So she started offering outsourcing services. And suddenly, she found herself much in demand and the owner of a thriving business. Her husband said that resigning from the consulting firm was the best thing she had done. But Parul knows that she left to be a consultant and had never dreamed she would become an entrepreneur. This was not a future she had planned or anyone had predicted. She is not sure if what has happened is good or bad.

If I had taken that job,
I would not be a successful
entrepreneur today.

Memory
Lane

If I had taken that job,
I would not be bankrupt today.

# Decisions are often rationalized in hindsight

In the battlefield of Kurukshetra, when Bhisma sees Shikhandi standing on Krishna's chariot, he lowers his bow. Taking advantage of this, Arjun who is standing behind Shikhandi lets loose a volley of arrows that pins Bhisma to the ground. Even though the great general of the Kaurav army cannot be killed, Arjun has managed to incapacitate him, increasing the chances of Pandav victory.

The Kauravs protest: the rules were breached, Shikhandi was a woman and no woman is allowed on the battlefield.

The Pandavs insist Shikhandi is a man: he was born with a female body but later in life, due to the intervention of a yaksha called Sthuna, had obtained male genitalia. Does that make Shikhandi a man or a woman? Is Bhisma wrong to assume Shikhandi is a woman? Is Arjun right to assume Shikhandi is a man? Since the outcome benefits the Pandavs, we can say Arjun's call is right, but the answer is anything but objective.

At the time of action, our decision is based on a set of assumptions. The assumptions may be wrong. Leaders have to constantly deal with uncertainty, give hope to the people even when nothing is clear. Decisions become good or bad in hindsight. We would like to believe that a decision is rational. More often than not, decisions are rationalized.

Often in business we take decisions based on how we interpret the situation, not being sure of whether the call we have taken will work or not. When it works, we are often taken by surprise. But the world at large demands an explanation. We are expected to prove that our decisions were strategic, not simply a fluke. To say that a certain victory was a fluke makes us nervous. Corporations reject this. Once the numbers come, the manager has to spend hours creating a story rationalizing his action so that everything looks as if it were part of a pre-conceived plan.

As the head of research and development, Dr. Sulabha prepares various types of snacks that the company then promotes in the market. Some succeed, some do not. Some become very successful. Each time the management asks Dr. Sulabha to give reasons why she feels a particular snack will be very successful and why they should invest in that product's development. She feels there is no one, except maybe a fortune-teller, who could actually give the right answer, but she is compelled to come up with satisfactory logic to comfort the management and ensure she gets funds, and keeps her job. At conferences she is often called to speak about her successful creations and the audience loves it when she tells them how she observed customer behaviour and strategized a product that eventually became a winner. The lectures would not be a hit if she were thanking providence or intuition for her best-selling snacks.

## If the decision is bad,
## the yajaman alone is responsible

A sage once asks a thief, "Why are you stealing?"

The thief replies, "I am poor. I need to feed my family. There is no other employment. I am desperate."

"Will your family bear the burden of your crime?"

"Of course, they will." Suddenly, not so sure of his own response, the thief decides to check. He asks his wife and son if they would bear the burden of his crimes and they reply, "Why? It is your duty to feed us. How you feed us is your problem not ours."

The thief feels shattered and alone. The sage then tells the thief, who is Valmiki, the story of Ram, as told in the Ramayan and compares and constrasts it with the story of the Pandavs from the Mahabharat.

Ram is exiled from Ayodhya for no fault of his, following the palace intrigues of his stepmother Kaikeyi. In the Mahabharat, the five Pandav brothers are exiled because they gamble away their kingdom, Indraprastha. In the Ramayan, Ram's exile lasts fourteen years. In the Mahabharat, it is an exile of thirteen years. In the Ramayan, there is no guarantee that at the end of the exile, Ram will be crowned king. In the Mahabharat, however, the Kauravs promise to return the Pandav lands on completion of the latter's exile.

While it is his father's request that he go to the forest, it is ultimately Ram's decision whether to obey his father or not. He decides to obey. He is no karya-karta to his father. He is a yajaman. He is never shown complaining or blaming Kaikeyi but is rather visualized as being stoic and calm throughout. In contrast, the Pandavs blame the Kauravs and their uncle Shakuni and are visualized as angry and miserable, even though they agree to the terms of their exile. They are compelled to obey the rules. Yudhishtir cannot bear the burden of being a yajaman, and agrees to play a game of dice, which costs him his kingdom, while his brothers assume the role of reluctant karya-kartas.

For Ram, Kaikeyi is no villain; he is no victim and certainly not a hero. A hero is provoked into action. A yajaman needs no provocation to act. Provocation makes action a reaction, turns a yajaman into a devata and a karta into a karya-karta. A yajaman takes his own decision. Ram has chosen to accept his exile. He could have defied the wishes of his father, and taken control of the throne, but he chose to obey. He takes ownership of his exile. The Pandavs constantly see their exile as an unfair punishment, a burden they are forced to bear. Perhaps that is why Ram (and not the Pandavs) is enshrined in temples.

A yajaman is one who does not blame anyone for any situation. He knows that his fortune and misfortune are dependent on many forces. Besides his knowledge, skills, experience and his power of anticipation, a lot depends on the talent of people around him—the market conditions and regulatory environment. He simply takes charge of whatever situation he is in, focusing on what he can do, never letting the anxiety of failure pull him back, or the confidence of success make him smug.

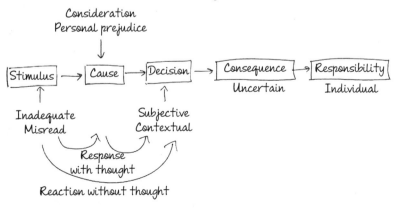

Upon the completion of their course in college, there is placement week. Jaideep gets two offers: one from an investment banking firm in New York and one from a leading trading firm in India. Jaideep chooses the job in New York, but the moment he lands there, news of recession fills Wall Street. Companies are forced to shut down or downsize. Jaideep finds himself without a job. As he flies back to Mumbai, he is angry and anxious. But he keeps reminding himself: it was his decision; no one forced him into the choice he made. He realizes that being a yajaman is tough.

## If the decision is good,
## the yajaman is the beneficiary

There is a king called Indradyumna, who after death goes to paradise to enjoy the rewards of his good deeds on earth. But, one day, he is told by the gods to leave paradise. He can come back only if he finds at least one person on earth who recounts his great deeds.

When Indradyumna reaches earth, he realizes that centuries have passed since his reign. The trees are different, the people are different, even his kingdom looks different. The city and temple he built no longer stand. No one remembers him. He visits the oldest man on earth, and goes to the oldest bird, but neither of them recall him. Finally, he goes to the tortoise, who is older than the oldest man and the oldest bird and the tortoise says he remembers Indradyumna because his grandfather had told him that a king called Indradyumna built the lake he was born in. Indradyumna, however, does not remember ever building a lake.

The tortoise explains, "You distributed many cows in charity during your lifetime, hoping to win a place in paradise, which you did. As the cows left the royal cowshed, they kicked up so much dust they created a depression which collected water and turned into a lake, becoming the home of many birds and fishes, worms and, finally, the home of my grandfather."

Indradyumna is pleased to hear what the tortoise has to say. So are the gods who welcome Indradyumna back to paradise. As Indradyumna rises to heaven, the irony does not escape him: he is remembered on earth for a lake that was unconsciously created, and not for the cows that were consciously given. He benefits not from his decisions but from the unknown consequences of his decisions.

Making decisions is not all gloom. It also yields positive results, sometimes even unexpected windfalls. Just as the yajaman is responsible for negative consequences, he has a right over positive consequences. It is this hope of unexpected positive consequences that often drives a yajaman.

---

Harish-saheb's factory provided a livelihood to Suresh who was able to give a decent education to his two sons, one of whom went on to become a doctor. Suresh was always grateful to Harish-saheb because before the factory was set up in the small town where he lived, he had been unemployed for over a year. When his son builds a hospital, Suresh insists that it be named after that 'giver of cows'—Harish-saheb. The Harish Nursing Home that serves the local community is, in this allegory, Indradyumna's lake. Harish-saheb's factory is long gone, replaced by a shopping mall.

---

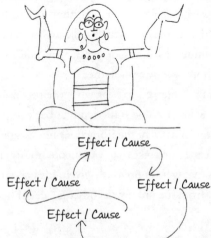

Karma means destiny; my past choices inform my current circumstance.

Karma means action; my current choice of action informs my future circumstance.

Effect / Cause

Effect / Cause

Effect / Cause

Effect / Cause

*Violence*

Without violence, there is no nourishment. Unless the mineral is consumed, the plant cannot grow. Unless the plant is consumed, the animal cannot grow. Physical growth demands the consumption of another. Only mental growth is possible without consuming another; but it is a choice humans rarely make.

# Business is violent

In the Mahabharat, the Pandav brothers inherit a forest, Khandavprastha, and want to build on it a great city, named Indraprastha, the city of Indra. So Krishna says, "Burn the forest. Set aflame every plant, every animal, every bird and every bee." When the Pandavs express their horror at the suggestion, Krishna says, "Then do not dream of a city."

Humans have the choice of outgrowing hunger like Shiva, or indulging hunger like Brahma. When we choose the latter, forests have to be cleared to make way for fields, and mountains have to be bored into to get to the minerals. The bull has to be castrated and turned into an ox, to serve as a beast of burden. The spirit of the wild horse has to be broken if it has to be ridden. Each of these actions has a consequence. This is violence and like all actions, even violence has consequences.

Culture is essentially domesticated nature. Different groups of humans have domesticated nature differently.

In Hindu mythology, the wild, naked and bloodthirsty goddess Kali and the gentle, demure and domestic goddess Gauri are one and the same. The former embodies the forest. The latter embodies the field. The former embodies prakriti. The latter embodies sanskriti. In between stands Brahma, performing the yagna that tames the wild and lays down the rules of man. Kali is the mother who existed before Brahma and his yagna. Gauri is the daughter, a consequence of Brahma's desire, forged by his yagna. Kali creates Brahma; Brahma creates and controls Gauri. He wants her to be obedient.

Forest
Wild
Khandavprastha
Prakriti

Kali

Gauri

Yagna

Field
Controlled
Indraprastha
Sanskriti

Humans have been constantly finding new and innovative ways of controlling nature. First it was the agricultural revolution. Then it was the industrial revolution. All these are violent attempts to gain more and more resources to satisfy the ever-increasing demands of humanity.

With each economic revolution, something has been sacrificed. The agricultural revolution had a negative impact on the lives of tribals who lived in forests and nomads who wandered freely over land. The industrial revolution displaced farmers, made them landless workers in factories and cities. The knowledge revolution means that jobs are being outsourced to foreign lands, benefitting the rich in the homeland, at the cost of the poor.

Violence is an intrinsic part of nature. In nature, animals kill plants and animals in order to survive. Animals compete with each other to survive. Humans have the ability to create a culture that can survive and thrive without needing to kill or compete. But this is not the path that is taken. Using force and fire, we tame nature. We expect Kali to turn into Gauri without resistance, but when she demands that Brahma turn into Vishnu, we mock her. In other words, we want to change the outer world (nature and society) rather than the inner world (mind). So long as we are not the victims of violence, we do not mind being the perpetrators of that violence. This is the human condition.

*Devdutt Pattanaik*

When Raymond bought a house in the suburbs ten years ago, he had a clear view of the sea and the mountains. But today his view is blocked by huge buildings, malls, roads and office complexes. He hates it. But then his wife pointed out, "Before our housing society was built I am sure there was a beautiful meadow here full of birds and butterflies. Someone would have been upset that a house was built here. But thanks to that decision by the builder, you and I have a home. Are you willing to sacrifice your house for the environment? Just as you wanted a house, other people also want a house and a job and so for them new houses, offices and roads have to be built. As long as society wants development, we have to be willing to sacrifice the environment. Everything has a price."

## Violence is not always apparent

Manu gives a tiny fish shelter in his pot, determined to save it from the big fish. As the days pass, the fish in Manu's pot keeps growing bigger and so Manu builds bigger pots to accommodate it. A point comes when the fish is so big that it has to be put in a pond, then a lake, then a river, and finally, the sea. The fish keeps growing and so to expand the sea, Manu asks the rain to fall. The rising sea causes flooding. The earth starts getting submerged beneath the waters. This is Pralay, the end of culture, the end of humanity, the end of all organic life.

Manu does not see the inherent violence in the creation of the pot. By saving the small fish he was denying the big fish their food. Another small fish was killed in place of the one rescued. The small fish does not stay small forever. It keeps growing. By seeking resources to provide for the ever-growing fish, he was destroying nature. At no point does Manu think the big fish can fend for itself. In trying to expand the pot to satisfy the demands of the fish, Manu ends up destroying the world.

Human society is built on the principle that the strong shall provide for the weak. The alternative is called jungle law and frowned upon. We also speak in terms of permanence: no aging but eternal existence, a growth curve that never wanes. The alternative is called being defeatist and philosophical. But in trying to provide everything for everyone, all the time, much is destroyed: cultures are destroyed, more of nature is destroyed, often for the noblest of intentions.

----

When the factory was built, the government insisted that schools and jobs be created to support the local tribal community. The factory owners did so diligently. Members of the tribal community were encouraged to study and learn new skills. They got menial jobs and they encouraged their children to study harder so that they could get more senior positions. Two generations down the line, the old tribal ways have all been all forgotten. The stories are no longer told. The rituals are no longer practised. A whole way of life has ceased to exist. Only anthropologists and museums have any memory of it. But the factory does not see itself as the destroyer of a culture; it simply sees itself as the harbinger of economic growth.

----

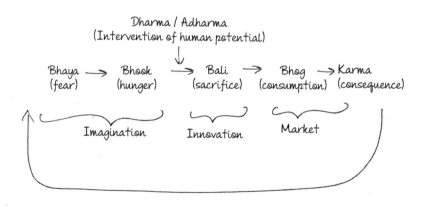

## Mental violence is also violence

The Bhagavat Puran tells the story of the river Yamuna that flowed past Vrindavan, the forest that was the favourite haunt of Krishna and his companions. One day, Krishna's elder brother wanted to take a bath and he asked Yamuna to come to him. Yamuna said, "But I cannot break the riverbanks. You must come to me." Balaram did not heed her words. He simply swung his plough and hooked it on the riverbank and dragged Yamuna, by the hair, to come towards him.

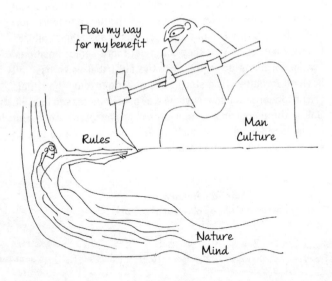

This story can be seen as a metaphor for canal irrigation. Unless the riverbank is broken, water cannot be made to flow into the fields. Violence helps man reorganize nature to his benefit. This is saguna violence, violence that can be seen. Violence associated with agriculture, industrialization and development is visible violence.

This story can also be seen as a metaphor for domesticating the mind. Our imagination flows in different ways as determined by our whim. Society, however, demands we control our imagination and function in a particular way, guided by rituals and rules. This is also violence: mental violence or nirguna violence, violence that cannot be seen. Every human wants to live by his rules but laws, values, systems, processes, regulations compel them to live by organizational rules. This results in invisible violence. Through mental violence, the human-animal is compelled to behave in a civilized way. At first there is resistance, but later it becomes a habit.

---

Radhakrishna loves Sundays when he wakes up at 10 a.m. and spends the day playing with his daughters, not shaving, not bathing, eating a late lunch, ending the day watching a movie with his wife on their home theatre system. Mondays he hates, as he has to get up at 6 a.m. and drive to work to be in office by 8 a.m., following up with team members, cajoling them or compelling them to finish their tasks so that he can give a favourable report to the client located in another time zone. It is a thankless job as he has to hear complaints from everyone around. But it pays well. On Sunday, Radhakrishna's Yamuna flows as per her will. On the rest of the days, it flows along the canals dug by others.

---

## Violence creates winners and losers

Harvest festivals are typically associated with the death of asuras: Diwali is associated with the death of Narak-asura, Onam and Diwali with the death of Bali-asura, and Dussehra is associated with the death of Mahish-asura.

The Purans state that asuras live in Pa-tala, the realm under the ground. All wealth in its most elemental form, be it plant wealth or mineral wealth, exists under the earth. Asuras will not let Lakshmi leave their realm; so the devas have to use force.

The sun (Surya) and the rain (Indra) pull out plant wealth, while fire (Agni) in the furnace and wind (Vayu) through bellows melt rocks and get metal out of ore. Activities such as farming and mining are thus described as war waged by devas against asuras. Unless the asura is killed, Lakshmi cannot be obtained.

Thank the gods for the sunlight and rain that compels the seed to sprout (worship deva)

Cut the crop to get the food (kill asura to get Lakshmi)

Kill the pest and uproot the weed (kill asura who has Sanjeevani vidya)

Wait for the ground to be fertile again before sowing the next crop (tapasya)

Lakshmi is called Pulomi, daughter of the asura-king Puloman, and Bhargavi, daughter of the asura-guru, Bhrigu. Shukra, the other asura-guru is her brother. In victory, the daughter of the asuras ends up as Sachi, wife of Indra, showering devas with pleasure, creating paradise with her arrival.

This story of the devas defeating the asuras is a narrative acknowledgement of the violence inherent in creating wealth. It refers to the visible violence of agriculture, mining, industrialization and every other extraction process.

It also reveals that with violence, there is bound to be a winner and a loser. Someone gains from the violence, and from that comes conflict. We adore those who pull wealth towards us rather than those who push wealth away from us. For humans, devas are gods, as their activities bring forth hidden wealth while asuras are demons, as they hide wealth in their subterranean realms.

---

The new road connecting the two major cities was going to pass through their farms. Twenty families would be displaced. The government promised them adequate compensation. For Mita-tai, this meant the end of all the things she had grown up with. The pond would go, as would the orchard. She would have to move to a new house maybe in the city with her son. She wanted to protest, but who would listen to an old lady. They would see her as an obstacle to progress. She cursed the government and all those who would ride on the road that took away her farm. But these were hollow curses of an unknown woman. According to the collector, the land belonged not just to her but also her two sisters and four brothers. All their names were on the deed, attested by her father's thumb impression. Only she had stayed in the village, with her husband, and taken care of the farm. Suddenly, all the relatives descended to take a share of the compensation. The deed was prepared thirty years ago before anyone had migrated and before the family quarrels began. Everyone had forgotten about the deed, until now. The government refused to pay any money until a consensus was reached. It took two years for that to happen. Mita-tai got only a fraction of what she felt she deserved. She went to her son's house, heartbroken. She died soon after. The road connecting the two cities brought livelihood to thousands of families. Indra had won his Sachi.

---

*Devdutt Pattanaik*

# Violence is culturally unacceptable if taking is not accompanied by giving

King Harishchandra had once promised to sacrifice his son, Rohit, if the gods cured him of a terrible ailment. The gods kept their end of the bargain, but Harishchandra hesitated about keeping his. He sought a way out, so his courtiers suggested he adopt a son. "The gods will not mind so long as you sacrifice a son," they said. So the king offered a reward of a hundred cows in exchange for a son he could adopt.

No one offered their sons; even orphans were not willing to be adopted, as they knew what was in store for them. But one priest, by the name of Ajigarta, agreed to sell his son, for he was very poor and he had three sons. "The eldest is dear to me. The youngest is dear to my wife. The middle one, we can spare." And so, the king adopted Ajigarta's middle son, whose name was Sunahshepa.

The time came to sacrifice Sunahshepa, but the royal priests refused to carry out the sacrifice of a human being. No one was willing to commit such a heinous act. "I will do it," said the boy's father, "if I am given another hundred cows."

This story fills us with horror, as the yajaman does not behave as a yajaman ought to. Rather than taking care of his subject, the king wants to sacrifice him for his own benefit. Rather than taking care of his son, the father wants to sell him for his own benefit. Both king and father are thinking only of their hunger. Both are indifferent to the needs of Sunahshepa.

In nature, it is acceptable that animals think only about themselves. But in culture, such selfishness is condemned.

We demand a fair exchange from people who have more

wealth and more power. Unfortunately, those who have more wealth and power are often in those positions because they have denied others any share of wealth and power. This is the root cause of rage and revolution. But things get complicated in defining what is fair. Is it fair for a king to kill another man's son to save his own? Is it fair for a father to sell one child to feed the others? Animals do not resent the predator who catches the prey, but humans do resent humans who exploit other humans.

The story of Sunahshepa draws attention to greed too. Ajigarta can plead poverty when he sells his son. But when the king offers to sacrifice his son, his motivation is not poverty anymore. What is acceptable when we are poor is not acceptable when we are not hungry. But then who decides who is poor and who is not. Certainly not a king who changes the definition of who his son is depending on convenience.

---

When Kanta could not pay back her dues, she gave her son Raghu away to a man called Pal who, in exchange, cleared her loan with the local moneylender. Raghu would work at Pal's house and be provided with food and shelter, but no salary. That was all right as Kanta could barely feed her six children. For Pal, transactions such as this enabled him to get labour at so low a cost that he was able to offer goods at prices that interested many foreign buyers. Kanta and Raghu are not even aware that there are laws against bonded labour and child labour. They are simply trying to survive, and Pal is taking advantage of the situation. Raghu, like Sunahshepa, lies in the twilight zone where neither parent nor state is able to take care of him.

---

*Devdutt Pattanaik*

# Violence becomes culturally acceptable when we take because no one gives

Indra, king of devas, once forbade the sage, Dadichi, from sharing the secret of the yagna with anyone. "If you do reveal the secret, your head will burst into a thousand pieces." But the twin sons of Surya, the Ashwini, were eager to learn this secret. When informed about the curse, the twins found a way out.

The Ashwini used their knowledge of medicine to cut off the head of Dadichi and replace it with a horse's head. Through the horse's head, Dadichi revealed the secret of the yagna. As soon as the revelation was complete, the horse head burst into a thousand pieces thus fulfilling Indra's curse. The Ashwini twins then attached the sage's original head and Dadichi came back to life.

Thus, the secret was transmitted. But a price had to be paid. The horse had to die. This could have been avoided had Indra allowed the free sharing of knowledge. But if knowledge was freely shared, would Indra be Indra, the king of devas and ruler of Amravati?

The devas believe that they have a right to what they have, that they are not obliged to give, like the inventor of an intellectual patent or the inheritor of a large conglomerate. This is disputed by those who believe wealth and knowledge need to be shared freely, that locking in wealth and building walls is the root of wars, deprivation and suffering.

For the devas, the asuras are barbarians who have to be killed for trying to steal the wealth that they have created. For the asuras, the devas are thieves who exploited resources that they never knew they had. Therefore, the battle between them is never-ending; each is convinced the other is unworthy and wrong.

Violence often happens when we take what others will not give. In Hindu mythology, the devas are often shown withholding treasures that other creatures want. This results in violence. The devas never lead a peaceful existence. Amravati is always besieged.

---

Kulapathi is an adviser to the government. He has advised the government against signing international patent laws. He believes that the creator does have the moral right to benefit from his creation. However, if he respects the creator's right, millions in his country will not get life-saving medicines. These will have to be imported at high cost and the government will be forced to provide subsidies and grants to make them available, which will ruin an already weak economy. Against immense international pressure, Kulapathi argues passionately about ignoring the rights of the creator. He feels he may be ethically wrong, but he is morally right. The rest of the world disagrees. Kulapathi is Dadichi who will ensure knowledge passes to the Ashwini, whether Indra allows it or not.

---

You must share your wealth with me. I did not know its value when it was with me.

Why? I worked for this wealth. I enhanced its value. Why should I share it with you?

*Devdutt Pattanaik*

# Exploitation is violence

Once, Lakshmi disappears from Swarga as the excesses of Indra disgust her. She dissolves herself in an ocean of milk. The devas decide to churn the ocean of milk to get Lakshmi back. They use Mount Mandara as the churning spindle and the serpent-king, Vasuki as the churning rope. But they realize they alone cannot churn the ocean; they need a counterforce. So they call upon their half-brothers, the asuras. The asuras agree as they are assured a share of the treasures that will emerge: the share is not clarified; no one knows what they will receive.

Many treasures emerge from the ocean: symbols of prosperity such as the wish-fulfilling tree, the wish-fulfilling cow, the wish-fulfilling gem; symbols of kingship such as the horse and the elephant; and symbols of pleasure such as wine, musicians and nymphs. The greatest treasure to emerge is amrit, the nectar of immortality.

The devas consume the amrit, and do not share it with the asuras, arguing that there was no agreement on what share would go to the asuras.

Rendered immortal, the devas now have an unfair advantage. They claim all the treasures of the sea and rise to the sky. The asuras are angry and they return to their realm under the earth. Never will they forgive the devas for their trickery. They will fight to repossess what was originally theirs, again and again for time immortal.

This story has confounded many Hindus, as conventionally, the devas are seen as gods, and are hence morally upright, while the asuras are demons, hence morally fallen. How can the gods trick and cheat?

The root of this confusion lies with the English words 'gods' and 'demons', used first by European orientalists, and the attribution of morality to devas. This distinction does not exist in the ancient Sanskrit texts, the Purans. In the Purans, both the devas and asuras are sons of Brahma, and represent different aspects of human personality.

The asuras sit over raw material, which unless extracted has no value. The devas bring value. If the devas did not come along, Lakshmi would stay dissolved in the ocean of milk. Because of the devas, Lakshmi becomes Sachi. Once she becomes Sachi, the asuras seek her back.

Often in a yagna, the tathastu is far greater than the svaha. The yajaman claims it as his right, since the yagna was his idea. But that does not stop the asuras from feeling they have been tricked or cheated. This sparks resentment and changes the mood of the yagna.

The asuras can be seen as the workers who work in industries which have been built using the money and knowledge of the devas. Who should be the beneficiaries of the fruit of their labour? Those who invested in the machinery and raw material, or those who laboured over it? The shareholders or the employees? The line of sight of the investor is different from that of the entrepreneur. What would construe a fair share? One party feels exploited and the other party feels fettered. Even the prajapatis disagree: Brihaspati sides with the devas and Shukra with the asuras.

The rishi saw the event from both points of view and realized there was no objective answer to the conundrum. The narrative of the battle between devas and asuras draws our attention to the violence inherent in a culture where both the haves and have-nots co-exist. At the same time, if there are no have-nots, there can be no haves.

When Hemadri returned home after completing his education, he spent hours looking at the financial statements of the family business. He realized that the family could easily pay the workers more wages and provide them with better facilities. His father and grandfather had a very different view altogether. "Before we came here, this place was a jungle with no employment opportunities. Now many have a job. If we overpay them, they will use that money to drink and beat their wives, which they do anyway with the meagre salaries we pay them. It will get worse. They will not turn up for work. They will become arrogant and demanding. Immigrant labour is no solution, as the locals will beat outsiders and drive them away. We have to control them and the best way to control them is by keeping them on a tight leash financially." Hemadri disagrees but as long as he is not in charge he has to keep his views on social justice to himself.

## Hoarding is violence

Like the never-ending conflict between devas and asuras, there is another conflict that is ceaseless: that between yakshas and rakshasas; also sons of Brahma who represent different aspects of human personality.

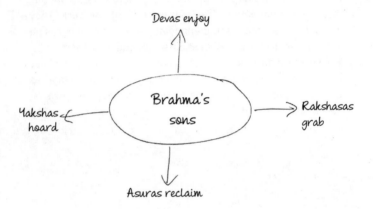

While devas do not share, the yakshas simply hoard. The latter are guardians of earth's treasures. They built the golden city of Lanka. The rakshasas led by their king, Ravan, drive the yakshas out of Lanka and lay claim to the city. The yakshas then seek refuge on the slopes of Kailas and build another city, called Alanka, more popularly known as Alaka. In Shiva's shadow, they feel safe.

The rakshasas are often mistaken for the asuras. They are two very different sons of Brahma. Asuras fight the devas to reclaim what they believe has been stolen from them. Rakshasas, on the other hand, do not believe in exchange; they simply take what they want.

The yakshas do not see hoarding as excess consumption

even though by hoarding, they deprive someone of wealth. The deprivation of wealth leads to starvation which, in turn, fuels violence.

It is ironical that both the yakshas and rakshasas worship Shiva who yearns for nothing. Yakshas keep hoarding because they are anxious to create enough wealth to avoid future starvation. The rakshasas keep stealing because that is the only way they know to gather food. The yakshas accuse rakshasas of laziness; the rakshasas accuse yakshas of greed. Each sees the other as villain and themselves as victims. Neither sees the fear, fuelled by imagination that makes them, and the other, behave the way they do.

---

The number of robberies in the neighbourhood has risen especially affecting senior citizens. Naturally, Mrs. Nagarkatti is scared. Her two sons are in America and her daughter is in Singapore. They call her every day and send her money by wire transfer. But in the house she is alone with one servant during the day and one at night. In the city there are many unemployed and underemployed young men and women who envy those who drive around in fancy cars, eat in fancy restaurants, and live in fancy homes. Every time they switch on the television they are enticed by advertising and lifestyles they cannot afford. One of them is Girish who visited Mrs. Nagarkatti's house to solve a small electrical problem. He noticed the diamonds in her ears and the gold bangle she was wearing. He asked her for 500 rupees. She called him an overcharging cheat, paid him only 200 rupees and complained to his boss. He wants to teach her a lesson. Or is that simply an excuse to justify his desire for the earrings and bangle that will allow him to experience all those fancy things he only dreams about. A lonely Mrs. Nagarkatti wants to move to an Alaka of her own, where she will feel safe in Shiva's shadow. Girish is on the verge of breaking the law and getting the diamonds and gold by force to his Lanka.

---

# Hunger is insatiable

Kubera, king of yakshas, once paid a visit to Kailas. There he saw Shiva's elephant-headed son, the corpulent Ganesha seated next to his father, and thought to himself, "Ganesha clearly loves food but Shiva cannot afford to feed him to his heart's content." So as a favour to Shiva, Kubera invited Ganesha to a meal. Ganesha accepted the invitation and entered Kubera's kitchen.

When the food was served, Kubera said, "Eat to your heart's content." Kubera regretted these words soon after, for Ganesha kept eating and eating. He ate everything that was in the kitchen and asked for more. Food had to be bought from the larder and then from the market. But Ganesha was still hungry. "More please," he said, raising his trunk. Kubera saw his treasures dwindling but there was no sign of Ganesha stopping. Finally, Kubera fell at Ganesha's feet realizing he was being taught a lesson.

Ganesha raised his trunk and said, "You really think food will satisfy hunger! Food fires the imagination, imagination enhances hunger. You seek to create more food, but food is finite and hunger infinite. My father seeks to destroy hunger. That is why I sit in his house, and not in your kitchen."

---

Sharda is thrilled when she learns that her contractor has to pay her more. She has a right to minimum wages. But now it has been two years, and the minimum wage she has been regularly paid is just not enough. With a regular income, she has been able to create a simple and secure lifestyle for her children. Unlike her, they have not spent their childhood going to bed hungry. Now they have dreams. They want things that she cannot afford to buy. Suddenly, what seemed like a lot of money two years ago seems paltry now. Unknown to Sharda, her contractor's son, Digvijay, was most happy when he got a salary that allowed him to buy a car; no more bus, train, or rickshaw rides to get to work. But now, two years later, he too is unhappy. He wishes he had a better salary so he could afford to hire a driver. Both Sharda and Digvijay are experiencing their hunger expanding because of imagination. Only introspection or tapasya will curtail it.

---

Indra's Amravati satisfies hunger. But Indra's name suggests that hunger is not physical—indriya, the term which gives rise to the name Indra, means the senses. Human hunger is not just the physical hunger of the stomach, but also the hunger of the senses. We yearn to pleasure the mind. We want entertainment, otherwise we are plagued by boredom, loneliness and angst. The hunger of the mind is far greater than the hunger of the body. That is why Indra needs not just the wish-fulfilling triad of Kalpataru, Kamadhenu and Chintamani but also needs the dance of the apsaras and the song of the gandharvas. So, no amount of wealth can satisfy him. That is why the rich aspire to be richer.

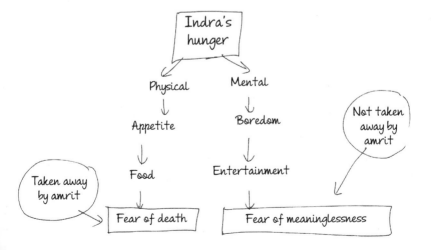

Civilized society speaks of generating and distributing enough wealth to satisfy the basic needs of people. We imagine that when these needs are met, there will be peace. But when basic needs are met, the mind craves the next level of needs. When that craving is not satisfied, there is conflict. Conflict will therefore never end, unless we address the root issue: craving itself. We can fill the stomach, but we can never satisfy the mind.

As long as the wound of Kama festers, there will be kalah, or conflict. Alakshmi, the goddess of kalah, is said to be Lakshmi's sister. There is conflict with and/or without wealth; only wisdom can rid us of kalah.

# Regeneration ensures sustainable wealth

Vishnu's most popular avatar is Krishna and Krishna's abode is called Goloka, the pastureland, which is full of cows that gather around Krishna who enthralls them with the music of his flute. These cows are not tethered and do not need to be. They give their milk to Krishna joyously, continuously and voluntarily.

Cows feed on grass which when eaten grows back, making grass a renewable raw material. The story goes that a pot containing amrit was placed on the grass a long time ago, enabling it to regenerate itself. With an assured and sustainable source of food, the cow is able to give a sustained supply of milk. This makes the cow and grass symbols of sustainable and regenerating resources, which makes them sacred and an integral part of Hindu and Jain rituals.

It is very easy to see this story literally: as an appeal for a vegetarian lifestyle, or as an endorsement for protecting cows. But the message is more symbolic: it reaffirms the need to secure a sustainable livelihood. This is why the gift of the cow, go-daan, is the greatest of gifts. It makes a man autonomous; he depends on no one for food (milk) or fuel (dung).

People are advised to give so many cows that the depression left behind as a result of the dust kicked up by the gifted cows turns into a lake which sustains more life. Go-daan is an appeal to create more means of livelihood that sustain more households. Go-hatya, or killing a cow thereby destroying a man's livelihood, is the greatest of crimes.

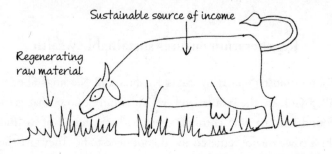

Sustainable source of income

Regenerating raw material

In Vishnu temples, Vishnu's mount, the eagle Garud, is shown holding a naga, or serpent, in his talons. It is an acknowledgement of the violence inherent in feeding. But the devotee is repeatedly told that the naga is immortal. The nagas slithered over the grass on which the amrit was kept and so they, too, possess the power to regenerate themselves like grass.

Vishnu is, thus, associated with the cow and the eagle, both of which consume what is in the mythological world considered renewable food sources. Regeneration is the key to sustainability. Words like regeneration and renewal are thus intrinsic to the yagna. They compensate for the harm done by violence.

---

Paresh-bhai noticed his son, Raghu, negotiating a price with the tempo owner. He saw the sense of triumph Raghu felt when he managed to bring down the price by another 10 per cent. Paresh-bhai, instead of congratulating Raghu, warned him, "If he runs out of business, we will lose a very good and honest transporter for our goods. In trying to improve your margin, you are destroying his very livelihood. He is already in debt. We need our vendors to survive and thrive so that they can support our business. If we grow at the cost of our vendors, we will do well for a short time, but then collapse. They will either shut down their business or rush to aid the competition as soon as it arrives." Paresh-bhai knows the value of regenerating serpents and regenerating grass.

---

*Devdutt Pattanaik*

## Restraint ensures regeneration

After harvest, for the land to restore its fertility, the farmer has to leave the land fallow. During spawning season, the fisherman must not go fishing so that he has enough fish to catch the rest of the year. Restraint is the key to regeneration and hence, also, sustainability.

Shiva is the god of restraint. He knows the secret of outgrowing hunger. Unlike Indra who only wants amrit, Shiva has the power to consume halahal, or the poison that accompanies amrit when the devas churn the ocean of milk. This is a metaphor for industrial waste that is a natural outcome of industrial activities. Indra does not care about the waste. But Shiva pays full attention to it; finding ways of containing, and even consuming it, so that the poison does not end up destroying the world. Without Shiva, the devas would not have access to amrit.

The devas, however, do not know the value Shiva brings to their lives, they remain wary of tapasvis. They prefer entertainment to introspection any day.

While the devas kill asuras, the asuras have the power to be reborn, thanks to Shiva. He gives them sanjivani vidya, the power to come back to life. The farmer may clear the forest, but sooner than later the weeds and floods come back. These weeds and floods play a key role in the regeneration of soil. Like the farmer who resents the weeds and floods, Indra resents the asuras who keep attacking Amravati at periodic intervals. He does not like Shiva helping them with sanjivani vidya. He imagines a world where every plant is a crop, existing solely for the satisfaction of his own hunger.

The asuras do tapasya to become more powerful, not wiser.

They worship Shiva as a source of power, and pay scant regard to his wisdom.

Only Vishnu knows the value of Shiva. He realizes that while performing a yagna externally to generate Narayani, the yajaman has to simultaneously perform tapasya internally and invoke Narayan if he wishes to have regenerating resources and a sustainable business.

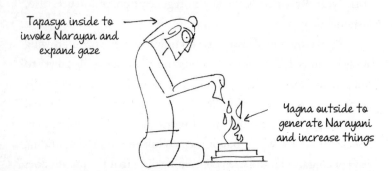

Tapasya inside to invoke Narayan and expand gaze

Yagna outside to generate Narayani and increase things

That is why the Veda keeps referring to the yagna-purush that has to be sacrificed during the yagna. While agni, the fire in the altar, burns resources externally, tapa, the fire in the mind, needs to burn the yajaman's ignorance. This needs to occur simultaneously with the ritual. Only then can there be intellectual growth along with emotional and material growth. If the yagna does not provoke intellectual and emotional growth in the yajaman, material growth will be indiscriminate and that will herald the floods of Pralay.

---

Pranita was always careful about money. She wanted to ensure that her children got a good education and lived a comfortable life. When she was forty, her fortunes changed. Her business started to boom. She began earning much more than her husband. "Now you can buy the jewellery that you

*Devdutt Pattanaik*

never bought," her husband said jokingly. Pranita smiled. She never bought jewellery not because she could not afford it but because she never desired it. Why should the availability of money change that about her? Why should extra resources make her change her comfortable lifestyle? Money for her was simply a tool of comfort. She did not value people, including herself, for the money they had. This mindset allowed Pranita to use her money to invest in more businesses, both high-risk and low-return ones. Before she knew it, she had become a small investment banker partnering with an NGO, giving out micro-loans, helping women in the slums near her house, all the while maintaining a comfortable lifestyle and ensuring her children were well educated and happy. Pranita's tapasya had enabled her not to be swayed by wealth, which enabled her to perform a better yagna than others.

---

# Restraint is violent

Rather than be encouraged to outgrow hunger through tapasya, humans typically seek to control hunger using external forces like rules and values. The path of Shiva is sidelined, as it is too mentally demanding, unpredictable, and uncontrollable. The more tangible path of Daksha and Manu is preferred.

Humans are the only living creatures with the power to contain fire in an altar, water in a pot, plants in a field, and animals in a barn. Likewise, we seek to restrain human behaviour by first defining what is acceptable behaviour and then taming the mind through force.

In nature, the strongest or most beautiful animal gets the mate. In culture, marriage laws are created to ensure everyone gets a spouse. In nature, the strongest and smartest gets the best and most food. In culture, property laws are created so that everyone, not just the strongest and smartest, can own things. The king is expected to enforce these laws; those who disobey risk punishment, exile and even death.

The Vishnu Puran tells the story of how Renuka, wife of the sage Jamadagni, is sexually attracted to the handsome king, Kartaviryarjuna, and how Kartaviryarjuna is fascinated by the magical cow, Nandini, that belongs to Jamadagni. Rules state that both wife and cow belong to the sage and everyone should respect the laws of marriage and property. Yet, neither Renuka nor Kartaviryarjuna is able to contain their respective desires. Renuka continues to dream of the handsome king while doing household chores and Kartaviryarjuna uses his military might to take Nandini by force despite Jamadagni's protests. Finally, Jamadagni orders his son Parashuram to pick up the axe, behead his mother and hack the greedy king to death.

Through rules and values, unacceptable desires and ambitions are contained and the imagination is encouraged to flow in a certain way. If the imagination resists, the axe falls. Modern society does not condone physical abuse, but considers it perfectly fine to terminate employment, or deny sustenance to a person caught cheating or stealing.

---

Vighnesh was very annoyed at the amount of paperwork and bureaucratic demands involved every time he took a loan. His father explained, "As long as you do business with your money, the authorities do not care so much. But once you take someone else's money, you have laws and regulations, and auditors and independent directors to ensure the money is not being misused. You have to continuously reassure the regulators that you are being honest and not rash." Vighnesh found this rather amusing. He realized the assumption was that a strict teacher would compel their students to have integrity. Since when did laws make people good? Rules and punishment would only encourage the greedy to be more cunning and manipulative to get around the system. Could the rules of society stop the craving to succeed at any cost?

---

Respect property rights

## Seduction

No one is obliged to receive what we give. No one is obliged to participate in the exchange. Not everyone needs to be compelled into desirable behaviour; customers and employees can also be charmed. Our enchantments can be a trick, a trap, a manipulation, or an expression of genuine affection that benefits all.

# Business is seduction

When King Dashrath's wives bear him no children and Lompad's kingdom suffers drought, both are advised to get Rishyashring to perform a yagna. Rishyashring cannot perform a yagna unless he is married and he will not get married because his father, Vibhandak, has raised him without any knowledge of women. In fact, his celibacy is suspected to be the cause of the childlessness and drought that plagues Dashrath and Lompad.

So Lompad's daughter, Shanta, is sent to the forest to seduce the young celibate sage. She spends hours with him, first pretending to be a sage herself, then gradually introducing him to the idea of gender, and finally by stirring sensual urges in him. Eventually, Rishyashring succumbs. He becomes Shanta's husband and she brings him to Lompad's city where he is welcomed with open arms. As a married sage, he conducts yagnas, one that brings rains to his father-in-law's drought-ridden kingdom, and another that grants Dashrath four sons, including Ram.

Business is about seduction. To increase market size, we have to seduce customers who have never used our product or service. To increase market share, we have to seduce customers away from the competition. Unless Rishyashring is seduced, neither Dashrath nor Lompad can have what they want.

---

For generations, Indian kitchens did not have pressure cookers. When they were first introduced in India, no one bought them. Although it cooked food faster and gave the cook more time to do other chores, people saw no value in a pressure cooker. They wondered what the cook would do with that extra time. Besides, experts were convinced that food did not taste as good. To change this mindset, a marketing campaign was created, which showed that a husband who loved his wife would buy her a pressure cooker, thereby making her life a little less stressful. And so went the seduction. Wives began to see pressure cookers as proof of their husbands' love. The sale of pressure cookers rose phenomenally. Today, pressure cookers are considered a necessity, hardly a luxury. Rishyashring had been seduced.

---

*Devdutt Pattanaik*

# He who satisfies hunger becomes desirable

This story comes from the Buddhist Jatakas. A young lad overheard a merchant say that a good entrepreneur would find opportunity even in a dead rat. The lad picked up a dead rat and wondered what opportunity there could be in it. While he was lost in thought, a cat approached him and began trying to catch the dead rat in his hand. "Give my cat that rat and I will give you a copper coin," said the owner of the cat. The lad pocketed the coin, and realized where there is hunger there is opportunity.

He thought of the grass-cutters who had to walk deep into the forest and got very thirsty on their way back, walking as they were in the afternoon sun carrying huge bundles of grass. So he greeted them midway, and offered them water from a pot he had bought with the copper coin he earned for the rat. In exchange for quenching their thirst, he asked each grass-cutter for a bundle of grass. Consequently, every day he got a bundle of grass without actually having to cut it. This he sold in the horse market, which earned him a copper coin every day.

Days later, he went to the merchant who had got him started by commenting about opportunities being present even in dead rats. He thanked the merchant for his wisdom. Hearing his tale of success, the merchant thought, "This young man is really smart and enterprising. An opportunity that I must not lose." He made the lad his son-in-law and before long, the lad was the most prosperous merchant in town, earning great wealth by satisfying the many hungers of the marketplace.

In the jungle, all animals, both predator and prey, come to the pond to quench their thirst. Business is about becoming the water body that attracts talent, investors and customers towards us.

---

When the new mall opened in Poonam Colony, Jayesh, the owner of the local kirana shop that sold provisions, became very nervous. He felt he would never be able to compete with the prices in the mall. Then he realized that his customers had small needs: a biscuit, bottle of soda, or a packet of snacks. It was too much to make the journey to the mall for such small items. Jayesh promised home delivery, however small the order. Before he knew it, he was flooded with calls. And invariably, the orders were large. The convenience of home delivery was something everyone had got used to in Poonam Colony and the mall could not break that habit despite great pricing. Jayesh's business was safe, at least for now.

---

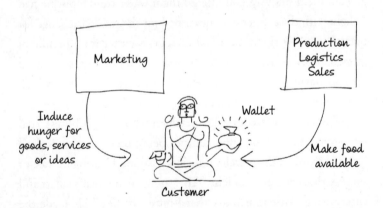

Marketing

Production
Logistics
Sales

Induce hunger for goods, services or ideas

Wallet

Make food available

Customer

*Devdutt Pattanaik*

# Many devatas need to be seduced

Every year, for the past six hundred years or so, in the temple of Jagannath in Puri, Orissa, a chariot of wood is made for the great chariot festival. A whole series of ceremonies precedes the building of the chariot. Worship is offered to the logs of wood, the instruments that will be used to carve it, and the carpenter who will turn the wood into the chariot. Before the satisfaction of the presiding deity, the wood, the carpenter and his instruments have to be pleased.

This behaviour is not an isolated practice. In household rituals, before the deity is worshipped, prayers and offerings are made to the implements of worship like the bell, the pot, the conch-shell and the lamp. In traditional dance performances, the dancers worship the stage, musicians, instruments and even the audience, before beginning their performance. Every link in the chain is worshipped; each one is sacred and significant.

In business, too, the yajaman depends on many devatas for his success. Each one needs to be acknowledged and paid obeisance to.

- There is the customer/consumer/client from whom the organization earns revenue.
- There is the employee through whom we get our work done.
- There is the employer who we report to, directly or indirectly, or via a dotted line.
- There are colleagues and co-workers without whose support we cannot do our task or achieve our target.
- There is the driver, doorman, office assistant and support staff who make life more comfortable.

There are devatas downstream and upstream and in lateral spaces. This presence of many devatas means that business is not merely a single yagna but a series of yagnas, or sattra. In fact, it is a maze of yagnas, each exchange interlocked with other exchanges, where the yajaman of one yagna serves as devata in another. We have to feed many devatas and many yajamans have to feed us.

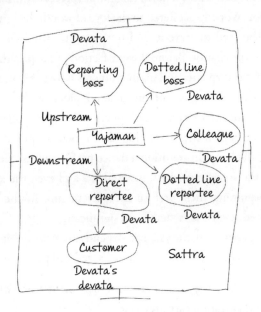

If the yajaman sees the business as a single yagna, he will frown upon personal goals if they are not aligned to the organizational goal. If he sees business as a sattra, he endeavours to make the organizational goal an outcome of everyone's personal goals.

As the manager of a pharma company, Manish knows that his success depends on many people. He knows that each of these devatas has separate needs. His team members, for example, work for their salaries and their bonuses. He makes sure that their appraisals are done on time. In fact, he is one of the few area managers who does appraisals proactively and does not have to be chased by the HR department for timely submission, indicating the value he places on that process. He knows that his boss needs the target plans and achievement sheets every Monday morning; he ensures these are emailed by Sunday evening. He regularly calls the HR and finance executives, even if he has no work, as he wants to build a relationship with them. This ensures that his work gets done smoothly and usually faster than others.

---

# Every devata has a devata of his own

In the Purans, when the devas are in trouble they turn to their father Brahma. When Brahma cannot solve their problem, he takes the devas to Vishnu. When Vishnu cannot solve the problem, Vishnu takes Brahma and the devas to Shiva. When Shiva cannot solve the problem, Shiva takes Vishnu and Brahma and the devas to the Goddess.

This is like an escalation matrix. When the problem cannot be solved at a particular level, one goes to the higher level. However, if the Goddess solves their problem, the next time the devas will bypass Brahma, Vishnu and Shiva and go directly to her. Yet, in every narrative there is no bypass. The structure is respected.

The Goddess does not really have to solve the problem of the devas. She has to solve the problem of Shiva. Why is he not able to solve Vishnu's problem? And Shiva has to solve Vishnu's problem. Why is Vishnu not able to solve Brahma's problem? Vishnu, in turn, has to solve Brahma's problem. Why is Brahma not able to solve the problem of the devas? Brahma has to figure out how to make the devas independent, so they can solve their own problems.

Every yajaman has a devata and every devata, in his capacity as yajaman, has a devata of his own. The yajaman has to solve not just the devata's issues but also figure out how to make him a better yajaman. Otherwise, there will be upward delegation and the gaze of the organization will be towards the boss, not the customer.

---

Felix has six people reporting to him. Each of them have ten people under them who, in turn, manage teams of about a dozen people who are client facing. Felix realized that while the tathastu of the company (revenue) came from the market, the tathastu of the employee (salary) came from the head office via the boss. Hence the gaze was typically upstream not downstream. People were more interested in boss management than customer management. To change this orientation, when he became head, Felix put the names of his six team members on a notice board in front of his desk. "You are the people who will help me succeed if I help you succeed," he told them in a team meeting. Next to each one's name he put down their individual short-term goals, first personal and then professional. Every week he would take time out to discuss these goals. As the months passed, he noticed each of his team members had similar sheets of papers on their notice boards, with the names of their respective team members. They were mimicking downstream what they were experiencing upstream. Were they being sincere or strategic? Felix did not know, but at least he ensured that his people focused a little more of their attention downstream than upstream.

## Every devata's hunger is unique

All devatas are placed in a puja room. The puja room is typically located in the northeast corner of the house. Just as the rising sun of the east indicates growth, the Pole Star of the north indicates permanence or stability. Accordingly, the puja room is grounded on the paradoxical and universal desire for growth on the one hand and stability on the other.

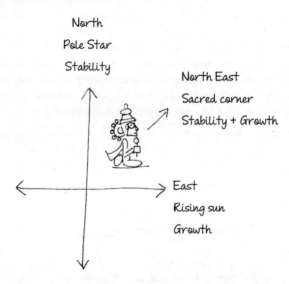

North
Pole Star
Stability

North East
Sacred corner
Stability + Growth

East
Rising sun
Growth

Each deity is kept facing the east, or the direction of the rising sun, a symbol of growth. The yajaman stands where the sun is supposed to be, suggesting that the yajaman hopes to bring in the same value as the sun, contribute to the growth of every devata he invokes. Also implicit in this arrangement is that the yajaman favours his devatas more than the rising sun. He chooses to face the devatas rather than the sun, acknowledging that without them he cannot grow.

Each deity is given his/her favourite food, flower and leaf. Shiva is given raw milk and bilva leaf while Krishna is given butter and tulsi leaf—recognition of the fact that while some needs like growth and stability may be common, every devata's tastes are unique. The more we customize the svaha, the more likely we are to delight the gods.

The puja room forces the yajaman to look at each devata as an individual, not as part of a collective. Often people look at organizations and forget they are sets of people. And we have to deal with people, not sets. Each person has his own strength and weakness, and he would like them to be at the very least acknowledged. A company with five thousand employees actually has five thousand individual vision statements. But typically, we focus only on one, that of the impersonal institution. This may be efficient, but it does dehumanize the organization.

---

At the annual internal conference, Inderjit is busy networking with the many partners of the consulting firm. When he meets Sorabh, he talks about the latest gadgets. When he meets Rathor, he talks about cricket. When he meets Satyendra, he talks about philosophy. When he meets Yamini, he talks about films. He never talks business with any of them. He knows that they are all tired of work and want to relax at parties. He also knows that they are bored and need entertainment. What better way to get entertained than talk on their favourite subject. Inderjit thus ensures every devata gets his favourite bhog. His performance is above average but not great. But his ability to make every partner smile has contributed to his being on the fast career track in the firm. The senior partner, Jagdish, who observes Inderjit making his moves, comments to Yamini, "If he can do the same with clients, we can be sure business will flow."

---

# Every devata matters
## depending on the context

In the nineteenth century, when European orientalists first translated Vedic hymns, they noticed that each hymn evoked different gods. Naturally, they assumed Hindus were polytheists like the Greeks. Then they noticed that each time a deity was being invoked he was treated as the supreme god, suggesting Hindus were monotheists like the Christians. This confused them. Were Hindus polytheistic or monotheistic? Monotheism was seen as superior back then and the British did not lose a single opportunity to embarrass Indians about their many gods.

Some suggested Hindus were henotheistic; they worshipped only one god but acknowledged the existence of others. Max Mueller came up with the term kathenotheistic, which means every god is treated as the supreme god turn-by-turn at the time of invocation. In other words, context determined the status of the god. In drought, Indra who brought rains was valued. In winter, Surya, the sun god was admired. In summer, Vayu, god of the winds was worshipped. And so it is in business. Everybody we deal with in business is important. But their importance soars as our dependence on them increases. Importance is a function of context, which makes all businessmen followers of kathenotheism.

In the puja ghar, the gods are classified under various categories; personal gods are called ishta-devata; household gods are griha-devata; family gods are kula-devata; village gods are grama-devata, and forest gods are known as vana-devata. Thus, there are different gods for different contexts: the personal, departmental, regional and the market. Each deity is of value only in a particular season or at a particular place. No one is of value everywhere and at all times. Each one plays a role in our life. Individually or collectively, they bring fulfilment to our existence.

---

Everybody in the Delhi office resents John. He has been hired by Sethji for a very good salary but does hardly any work. He spends all day surfing the net, leaves office early and spends his evenings out in clubs, partying with the rich and famous. When questioned by his rather conservative head of accounts, Sethji says, "When I have work with government agencies, I ask John to make the calls. Because he is a foreigner, doors open for him. I get appointments. He starts the meeting and I finish it. And because of his clubbing, he invariably knows the sons and daughters of ministers and other influential people. The officers try to impress him by ensuring the work gets done without too much hassle. So you see, John is like my umbrella. Not useful everyday but certainly of great value on a rainy day. He is worth every penny I pay him."

---

Ishta-devata
(Customer)

Griha-devata
(Subordinate)

Grama-devata
(Regional manager)

Kula-devata
(Head of Department)

# Not all devatas are equal

Once, a child defeated Taraka, a great asura. The child had six heads, rode a peacock, had the symbol of a rooster on his banner and a lance in his hand. As the bearer of such potent symbols of virility, he was clearly no ordinary child. Who was he?

"He is my son," said Gauri, "I merged six babies into one to create this divine warlord." "He is our son," said the six Krittika stars. "Each one of us nursed those six babies since their birth." "He is my son," said the Saravana, the marsh of reeds, "I provided the fuel for the fire that transformed six seeds in a river into six babies on a lotus." "He is my son," said the river-goddess, Ganga. "My flow turned a single seed into six." "He is my son," said Vayu, the wind god, "I reduced the heat of the single seed otherwise it would have scorched dry the rivers of earth." "He is my son," said Agni, the fire god, "only I had the power to catch that fiery seed that Vayu cooled and Ganga turned to six." "And who caused the seed to be released from the body of Shiva? It was me! I am the mother of this warrior," said Gauri again.

Gauri, Krittika, Saravana, Ganga, Vayu and Agni, six deities claimed to be the mother of the child-warlord, and each was right from their own point of view. To stop the bickering, the contribution of each of these 'mothers' was acknowledged by giving the child many names: Kumara for Gauri, Kartikeya for the star-goddesses, Saravana for the reed marsh, Gangeya for the river-goddess, Guha for the wind-god and Agneya for the fire-god. This made everyone happy. A special prayer was reserved for the father, Shiva, from whose body came the seed of which the child was a fruit.

We depend on the entire team for its outputs. Every member

of the team is a devata. But in teams there are always idea generators and idea implementers. It makes good sense for the yajaman to distinguish between the two. While idea implementers are essential, the idea-generator is critical.

---

When their advertising campaign won a prestigious global award, Rima threw a huge party where she personally thanked everyone from the planning team to the creative team and media team. Without their contribution, this would never have happened. When the crowds were gone, Rima walked up to Milind, the quiet creative head. She knew it was he who had sold the bold concept to the client. He was the cornerstone of the project. Everyone was essential; but Milind was critical, the idea-generator, the Shiva whose seed was incubated in many wombs to create Kartikeya.

---

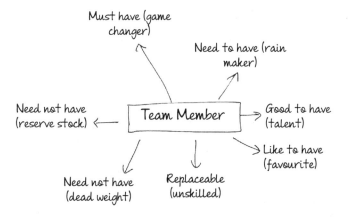

## Seducing multiple devatas is very demanding

Dealing with many devatas is not easy. Chandra, the moon god, was a failure. Draupadi, the heroine of the epic Mahabharat, was a partial success, but Krishna was the most successful of all.

Though Chandra marries the twenty-seven daughters of Daksha, he prefers only one—Rohini. Only a threat from Daksha makes Chandra pay attention to his other wives. But he gives his svaha reluctantly, waning as he moves away from Rohini and waxing when he comes close to her.

By contrast, Draupadi treats all her five husbands equally and constantly tries to satisfy each of them. Even though she yearns for Arjun, her favourite, and finds Bhim most useful, she never forgets that as the shared wife of the five Pandavs she has to treat all husbands equally. To ensure there is no jealousy, she is faithful to each husband for a full year and then passes through fire, regenerating her body, before moving on to the next. She pays careful attention to everyone's hunger, making herself so dependable that none of them can bear the thought of losing her. This is not easy as every husband's hunger is different: Yudhishtir, the eldest, loves conversations on matters of state; Arjun enjoys being praised for his archery skills; Bhim loves food; Nakul loves being admired for his beauty; and Sahadev enjoys being silent. And yet, despite all her efforts, when it comes to protecting her, all the brothers fail—both individually and collectively—when they do nothing as she is being publicly abused by the Kauravs.

In the Bhagavata, Krishna dances with many milkmaids or gopikas in the forest of Madhuvan. Every gopika thinks he dances exclusively for her, so well does he meet all their demands. For that reason, the dance of Krishna and the gopikas forms a perfect circle, with each one equidistant from him despite their varied personalities. This circle is called the rasa-mandala. Here, no gopika resents the other. Just as Krishna treats them as devatas, they give due respect to him, their yajaman and strive to make him happy by ensuring the rasa-mandala includes everyone. Krishna focuses on the personal goals of the gopikas, and the gopikas—by focusing on the personal goal of Krishna—end up meeting the organizational goal.

| | Gives svaha to all | Gets tathastu from all |
|---|---|---|
| Chandra | ✗ | ✗ |
| Draupadi | ✓ | ✗ |
| Krishna | ✓ | ✓ |

Seduction is truly successful only when the devatas strive to satisfy the hunger of the yajaman. The point is for the employer to get the employee to give his best voluntarily, and vice versa. When we rely on rules, regulations, reward and reprimand to get our work done, it means we want to domesticate our devatas, rather than seduce them. It means they are doing work reluctantly not joyfully.

---

Ever since Rehman took over as the manager of the restaurant, there has been a marked change in the energy of the place. The sweeper does not need to be supervised, the waiters do not need to be ordered around, and the cook does not need to be instructed. Everyone is taking ownership of their duties and giving their best. This is because Rehman never talks about tasks and targets, except on Saturdays. The rest of the week, he checks if everyone is happy doing their job, satisfied with what they have achieved. He nudges them gently when they slack, never admonishing or shaming them. With Rehman around, they feel less like servants and more like owners. Rehman does not see work as a fulfilment of contract; he has linked their work with their self-esteem and their self-worth. The workplace energizes everyone and so they contribute beyond the call of duty.

---

# Seduction needs to satisfy both parties

Seduction is an essential component of the yagna. Who does the seduction benefit: only the yajaman or also the devata? When the seduction benefits only the yajaman and leads to material growth for him, the yajaman is Menaka. When the seduction benefits both yajaman and devata and also generates intellectual and emotional growth, the yajaman is Mohini.

Menaka is an apsara sent by Indra to distract the tapasvi Kaushik from his austerities. Menaka dances in front of the aspiring hermit and compels him to open his eyes. Menaka thereby successfully seduces Kaushik much to Indra's delight. On Kaushik's failure rests Indra's success.

Mohini is the form that Vishnu takes when the devas and asuras fight over the distribution of amrit they have churned out of the ocean of milk. She offers to distribute the nectar fairly and, spellbound by her charms, everyone is eager to believe she will be fair. But she is not. It is some time before the asuras realize that Mohini pours the amrit selectively down the throat of only the devas. By then it is too late. The devas become so powerful that they drive the asuras back to the nether regions and rise to the sky laying claim over every treasure that has risen from the ocean of milk.

On the face of it, it seems a simple story where Vishnu as Mohini tricks the asuras and favours the devas. What is left unsaid, though, is more interesting. By giving amrit to the devas, Mohini liberates them from physical death but condemns them to mental boredom. For life has no purpose, and the devas end up chasing thrills and excitement to fill their waking hours.

By denying amrit to the asuras, Mohini grants the asuras a sense of purpose. They feel like victims and are determined to get back what the devas stole from them. The devas can kill the asuras but sanjivani vidya resurrects them, so they keep coming back, again and again, denying the gods the pleasure of peace.

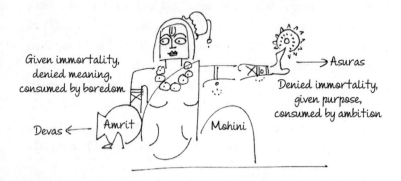

Given immortality, denied meaning, consumed by boredom

Devas ←— Amrit

Mohini

→ Asuras

Denied immortality, given purpose, consumed by ambition

The asuras do tapasya for power; the devas do yagna for pleasure. Asuras crave justice only for themselves. Indra craves only his own happiness. Neither sees the other, or anyone else. Vishnu seeks to provoke thought in the sons of Brahma. For only when they stop fighting and are at peace can he go back to sleep.

The promotion was given to Radha and not to Maithili. Maithili was very angry and accused Devesh of favouritism. Or was it a sexual favour? Devesh was annoyed by the accusation but did not get upset. He was well aware that both ladies were extremely competitive besides being competent. Neither liked losing which made them star performers. Unfortunately, he could not promote both of them. It was clear that Maithili would resign and join a competitor. In Devesh's view, both girls won. Radha got her promotion and Maithili got a chance to expand her experience by working with new colleagues. Radha would have to learn how to deal with old colleagues who would resist reporting to her. Maithili would have to learn how to deal with new colleagues who would see her as an outsider. Like the devas, Radha would gradually stop feeling obliged to Devesh, and like the asuras, Maithili would never stop resenting him.

---

## Sometimes, the yajaman also needs to be seduced

Only a son of Shiva can kill Indra's great enemy, the asura-king Taraka. But Shiva has no hunger, no desire to father a child. He seeks no tathastu and offers no svaha. A desperate Indra sends legions of apsaras along with Kama to seduce Shiva. But Shiva's eyes remain firmly shut. The arrows of Kama have no effect on him. In fact, an irritated Shiva opens his third eye, releasing a missile of tapas that reduces Kama to ash.

Vishnu then enlists the help of the Goddess who takes the form of Kamakshi. Kamakshi is another name for Gauri. In Tamil folk literature Gauri is often called the sister of Vishnu. She approaches Shiva not as a damsel but as a devotee, determined to marry him and have his offspring. Impressed by her devotion, Shiva marries her and together, they produce Kartikeya who becomes the commander of the devas and goes on to kill Taraka.

In lesser-known versions, Vishnu as Mohini makes Shiva father a son known variously as Manikantha, Sastha or Aiyanar, the great celibate warlord who defeats many asuras and is much revered as a folk god in South India. Shiva rejects Indra's overtures but accepts those of Kamakshi and Mohini. Why so? Indra wants Shiva to be seduced for his own pleasure. Kamakshi and Mohini want Shiva to be seduced for the benefit of the world.

Mohini and Kamakshi transform Shiva, the hermit, to Shankar, the householder and lead him from the icy peaks of Kailas to the riverbank city of Kashi, the great marketplace.

But Shiva has no need for the marketplace. He is described as digambar, the naked one. He wears nothing. At best, he is wrapped in animal hide and smeared with ash. Vishnu, on the other hand, is draped in silks, anointed with sandal paste, and bedecked with garlands of fragrant flowers and leaves, and necklaces of gold and pearls. Implicit in Vishnu's costume is the existence of different communities: farmers, spinners, weavers, dyers, miners, smelters, smiths, jewellers and traders. In other words, Vishnu's form symbolizes the idea of sanskriti. Vishnu sees the market as a great place to engage with humans. Every yagna is a great opportunity to pay attention to other people's hunger.

Indra does not care for the hunger of others. For him, the yagna exists only for his pleasure. Daksha looks at the yagna merely as a process, a duty, or burden to be borne. To make Indra and Daksha widen their gaze, Shiva's intervention is needed. Only he can teach them the futility of seeking happiness through Lakshmi alone. Happiness will come only when material growth is accompanied by intellectual and emotional growth. And this can only happen when they start paying attention to the hunger of the devata, expand their brahmanda to include that of others and make themselves dependable. And so, Kamakshi appeals to Shiva's grace. Shiva may not need the marketplace, but the marketplace needs him.

Business is not merely an instrument to generate wealth for shareholders or provide services to customers; it builds an ecosystem that provides opportunities to entrepreneurs and creates markets that benefit society at large. Indra sees industry as an end in itself. Vishnu sees industry as an essential ingredient of society at large. For the perfect marriage between industry and society, a perfect balance needs to be maintained between consumption and restraint. While the devata's hunger needs to be indulged, the yajaman needs to work on outgrowing his hunger. That is why Shiva needs to descend from Kailas and be in Kashi.

A similar transformation can be found in Buddhist literature when the wise Buddha of Thervada Buddhism (original school; popular in Sri Lanka and Southeast Asia) is gradually transformed into the form of the compassionate Bodhisattva of Mahayana (later school; popular in China). Buddha is serene and distant with eyes shut, while the Bodhisattva is more engaging and participative with his eyes open and his many hands reaching out to comfort people. Often Bodhisattva is visualized as the female Tara, or accompanied by her. In Vajrayana Buddhism (latest school; popular in Tibet and Bhutan), the two are often in passionate embrace indicating the union of intellect and emotion. In many ways, Tara performs the function of Kamakshi and Mohini. She is the glue of sensitivity and compassion that binds the hermit and the marketplace.

It is no accident that Shiva, who outgrows hunger, gets a wife who is also known as Annapoorna, the provider of food. He embodies the human potential and she embodies nature's resources. Both need to be realized.

Radhakant loves manipulating people, making them feel wanted, and getting them to do exactly what he wants. Many people fall for it, until one day they realize they have been used and leave the organization with a broken heart. Radhakant is Indra who hires Kama and Menaka to get his job done. He does not care for others. His brother Lakshmikant watches this and wonders where Radhakant's desire to manipulate people comes from. All his life Radhakant tricks people and gets his way. He calls this "winning". He is convinced he is right and everyone else is wrong. He wonders why his wife and son constantly fight with him; they refuse to be manipulated by him and get angry when he tries. So many times, Lakshmikant has thought of leaving the firm and working on his own, away from Radhakant's pettiness. But that would be like going to Kailas and finding peace in isolation. He feels he has to stay in Kashi, and help his brother find happiness. The more he watches people get manipulated by Radhakant the more he realizes how desperate people are for affection and love. They let themselves get entrapped and hunted by wily predators, and then feel like victims and martyrs. This realization makes him occasionally smile.

*Churning*

An organization is made up of various forces: production, marketing, sales, audit, legal, finance, logistics and so on. There are times when each force has to dominate and times when each has to submit. In a churn, one needs to know when to let go otherwise the act of churning turns into a tug-of-war where the organization becomes a battleground.

# The organization is ultimately a set of people

Organizations are like the sky; it does not really exist. It is a visual illusion. What really exists are the taras or stars and the grahas or planets (celestial bodies, actually), and the relationships between them as perceived by observers. Sky-gazers are actually stargazers. Taras and grahas are people who make up the organization. The taras are the nameless workers while the grahas are the talent who determine the fate of the organization.

No one knows the names of individual taras; they are identified through the constellation they belong to, such as the twelve solar houses (rashi) or the twenty-seven lunar houses (nakshatra). Stars are natural, constellations are not, yet it is constellations that enable us to map the sky and make sense of it. Likewise, in an organization, less value is given to individual workers and more to the group they belong to. An individual worker is not as important as the group he belongs to, as he is viewed as a replaceable set of skills. Teams, regions and departments are artificial divides, yet they are critical for the organization's efficiency and effectiveness. Replacing a team is not easy.

Every graha matters. Each one has a name and a detailed personality. Using information available in Jyotisha-shastra or Vedic astrology, people who make a difference to an organization can be classified as:

* Ravi, the sun, who is radiant and attracts attention wherever he goes.
* Soma, the moon, who is emotional and moody.

- Mangal, or Mars, who is an aggressive go-getter.
- Budh, or Mercury, who is an excellent communicator, slippery and silver-tongued.
- Brihaspati, or Jupiter, who is rational and relies on data.
- Shukra, or Venus, who is intuitive and relies on gut feeling.
- Shani, or Saturn, who procrastinates and obstructs.
- Rahu, or the eclipse-causer, who is secretive and hates being transparent.
- Ketu, or the comet, who is restless and spreads anxiety.

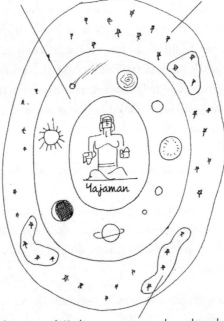

Grahas = planets = Talent whose individual personalities impact an organization

Tara = stars = Talent whose individual personalities do not impact the organization

Yajaman

Rashi/Nakshatra = constellation = groups or departments or teams, where collective performance matters not individual personality

*Devdutt Pattanaik*

A graha is a talented devata demanding his place in the grand pantheon of the organization. In conjunction with some groups, a celestial body has a favourable impact; in others, the relationship can be disastrous. Likewise, some talents do well in a particular group and not so well in another. A manager may do well in the audit team but not in the business development team. A manager may do well as long as he is dealing with marketing matters but he may fail in matters related to logistics.

What matters most is the relationship of all the grahas with each other. If individual talents do not get along with each other, if business unit heads do not collaborate with each other, it could lead to a leadership crisis, which does not bode well for the organization.

Everybody yearns for an optimal alignment of grahas, rashis and nakshatras. This is colloquially called jog, derived from the word yoga. A yajaman who is able to design such optimal alignments on his own, or makes the best of whatever alignment he inherits, is considered a magician, a jogi. Sometimes he is also called a 'jogadu', the resourceful one, admired for his ability to improvise or do 'jugaad' with the resources at hand.

---

Prithviraj is the head of a telecom company with forty thousand employees. He feels like Surya, the sun, with the whole world revolving around him. Each client-facing executive is like a star that is part of a constellation which, in turn, is part of a larger constellation. He can see them but he rarely engages with them. His daily interaction is with about fifteen people who make up his core team. They are his grahas. Through them, he exerts influence over all stars, across the sky, which is his marketplace. He is aware of each graha's personality; who is restless, who is aggressive, who is moody and who gets along with whom. He works with them, helping them enhance their positives and work on their negatives, to get the fine balance that will give him the success he so desperately wants. He wants a finance head who is firm yet gentle, a marketing head who is flamboyant yet level-headed, and an operations head who is both people and numbers driven. He is getting there.

---

Are these talents aligned well with reference to each other? →

← Is the talent team aligned well to the market?

↑ Are the talents aligned well to respective departments?

*Devdutt Pattanaik*

## Every organization is a churn

When the devas wish to churn the ocean of milk, Vishnu suggests they take the help of the asuras, for a churn cannot work without an equal and opposite counterforce. In business, the organization is the churn while the market is the ocean of milk in which Lakshmi is dissolved. The various departments of the organization and members of the leadership team serve as force and counterforce, respectively.

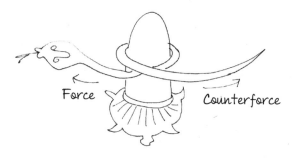

Force — Counterforce

Vishnu alone knows when to pull and when to let go, how much to pull and how much to let go, who should pull and who should let go. To ensure that the churning is happening correctly, he holds four tools in his four arms. This is why he is also called Chaturbhuj, the one with four arms. Each tool symbolizes one of the four things to keep in mind when supervising any project.

- The conch-shell trumpet stands for clear communication. The yajaman needs to clearly communicate his expectations to his team.
- The wheel stands for repetition and review. The yajaman needs to appreciate that all tasks are repetitive and need to

be reviewed periodically.

- The lotus is about appreciation and praise. It complements the club.
- The club stands for reprimand and disciplinary actions. It complements the lotus.

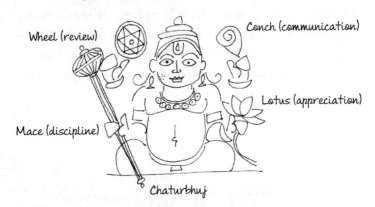

Wheel (review)
Conch (communication)
Lotus (appreciation)
Mace (discipline)
Chaturbhuj

The conch-shell and lotus are instruments of seduction. The wheel and the club are instruments of violence. The yajaman needs to know when to be nice and when to be nasty, depending on the context, so that ultimately, work gets done.

When Lakshmi is not forthcoming, Vishnu knows that the churn has been damaged: either someone is pulling when they are not supposed to or someone is refusing to let go. It is then that he uses the four tools in the right proportion, as the situation demands.

---

Arvind has a peculiar style of management that few in his team have deciphered. When everyone is together, he enjoys visioning and planning and ideating. He publicly announces individual and team successes and takes people on celebratory

*Devdutt Pattanaik*

lunches. When he is reviewing his team members, or pulling them up for indiscipline or lack of integrity, he only does it in private. By doing the positive things in public, he amplifies the positivity in the team. By doing the negative but necessary things in private, he avoids spreading negativity.

---

# If strategy is the force, then tactic is the counterforce

Vishnu rides an eagle or garud, and rests on the coils of a serpent or sarpa, which is to say he has both a wide view, as well as a narrow view. His vision is both long-term and short-term. The big picture is garud-drishti, or the bird's-eye view or strategy. The more detailed, context-specific picture is sarpa-drishti, or the serpent's eye-view or tactic.

Both these views are demonstrated in the Ramayan. Dashrath's second queen, Kaikeyi, asks him for the two boons he promised her long ago: that Ram, the eldest son and heir, be sent into forest exile for fourteen years, and that her son, Bharat, be made king instead. When Dashrath informs his sons about this, Ram immediately agrees to go into exile but Bharat does not agree to be king.

Ram agrees because he knows the immediate impact of his decision: the people of Ayodhya will be reassured that the royal family always keeps its promises, however unpleasant. Bharat disagrees because he knows the long-term impact of his decision: no one will be able to point to the royal family as being opportunists and thereby justify future wrongdoing. By demonstrating sarpa-drishti and garud-drishti, Ram and Bharat ensure the glory of the Raghu clan.

In contrast, neither view is demonstrated in the Mahabharat. Satyavati refuses to marry the old king Shantanu of the Kuru clan unless she is assured that only her children become kings of Hastinapur. Shantanu hesitates, but his son, the crown prince, Devavrata, takes a vow of celibacy, demonstrating neither sarpa-drishti nor garud-drishti.

In the immediate-term, both Shantanu and Satyavati are happy. But in the short-term, the kingdom is deprived of a young, powerful king. The old king dies and for a long time the throne lies vacant, waiting for Satyavati's children to come of age. In the long-term, this decision impacts succession planning. The Kuru clan gets divided into the Kauravs and the Pandavs, which culminates in a terrible fratricidal war.

Market has to be developed.
We need to invest.

We need to achieve our quarterly target,
and get high returns on every investment.

When asked why he needed a chief operating officer, Aniruddh told the chief executive officer that he needed someone downstairs to pay attention to quarterly targets and someone upstairs to pay attention to the long-term prospects of the company. "I want the CEO to think of the five-year plans, product development and talent management, not waste his time thinking of how to achieve today's sales." Aniruddh knows that there will be tension between the CEO and COO, as the COO will have more control over the present yet will have to report to someone whose gaze is on the future. This tension between the sarpa and the garud was necessary if Lakshmi had to keep walking into the company for a sustained time.

# If creativity is the force, then process is the counterforce

Kama is the charming god of desire and creativity. He rides a parrot and shoots arrows of flowers rather indiscriminately, not bothering where they strike. Yama is the serious god of death and destiny, associated with the left-brain. He keeps a record of everything and ensures all actions are accounted for.

If Kama is about innovation and ideas, Yama is about implementation and documentation. Kama hates structure. Yama insists on structure. Kama is about play. Yama is about work. Human beings are a combination of the two.

Vishnu is a combination of both Kama and Yama. His conch-shell and lotus represent his Kama side, as everyone loves communication and appreciation, while his wheel and mace represent his Yama side, as everyone avoids reviews and discipline.

In folklore, there is reference to one Shekchilli who dreams all the time and never does anything. He is only Kama with not a trace of Yama. Then there is one Gangu Teli, who spends all day doing nothing but going around the oil press, crushing oilseeds. He is only Yama with not a trace of Kama. Then there are Mitti ka Madhav and Gobar ka Ganesh, characters who neither dream nor work, and are neither Kama or Yama. They do what they are told and have neither desire nor motivation. Finally, there is Bhoj, the balanced one, who knows the value of both Kama and Yama, and depending on the context, leans one way or the other. Bhoj is Vishnu.

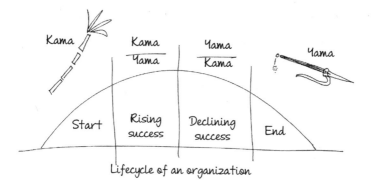

Lifecycle of an organization

In the early phases of an organization, when ideas matter, Kama plays a key role as the vision of the yajaman excites and attracts investors and talent to join the team. In the latter stages of an organization, when implementation is the key to maximize output, Yama starts playing an important role; more than dreams, tasks and targets come to the fore. When creativity and ideas cease to matter, and only Gangu Teli is in control, the organization lacks inspiration and is on its path to ruin. Thus, the proportion of Kama and Yama plays a key role in the different phases of a company.

---

When the team met to brainstorm, Partho always came across as a wet blanket. As soon as an idea was presented, he would shoot it down by citing very clear financial or operational reasons. His boss, Wilfred, would tell him to keep implementation thoughts for later, but Partho felt that was silly as the most brilliant projects failed either because of inadequate funding or improper planning of resources. He felt ideation should always be done with the resources in mind. Partho comes across as a Yama who always looks at numbers and milestones, especially when compared with his very popular boss, Wilfred, who is clearly a Kama. But he is actually a Bhoj, highly creative, but lets the reality of resource availability determine the limits of creativity.

---

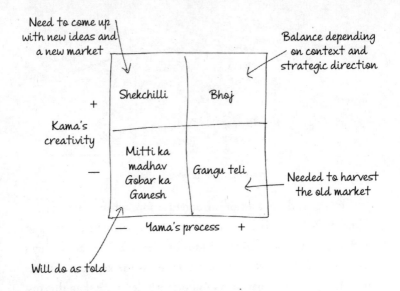

Need to come up with new ideas and a new market

Balance depending on context and strategic direction

+ Kama's creativity

−

Shekchilli

Bhoj

Mitti ka madhav Gobar ka Ganesh

Gangu teli

Needed to harvest the old market

− Yama's process +

Will do as told

## If ambition is the force,
## then contentment is the counterforce

Growth drives most organizations. Along with growth comes change, and change is frightening. In the pursuit of growth, one must not lose sight of the stability of things already achieved.

The most common example of force and counterforce in mythology are the devas and asuras. The devas are not afraid of death but they are afraid of losing everything they possess. On the other hand, the asuras are afraid of death but have nothing to lose, as they possess nothing. This makes devas insecure and the asuras ambitious.

The devas want to maintain the status quo whereas the asuras are unhappy with the way things are. The devas want stability, the asuras want growth. The devas fear change and do not have an appetite for risk while the asuras crave change and have a great appetite for risk. The devas enjoy yagna, where agni transforms the world around them; the asuras practise tapasya where tapa transforms them, making them more skilled, more powerful, more capable. The devas enjoy Lakshmi, spend Lakshmi, which means they are wealth-distributors, but they cannot create her; the asuras are wealth-generators hence her 'fathers'. An organization needs both devas and asuras.

They need to form a churn, not play tug of war. In a churn, one party knows when to pull and when to let go. Each one dominates alternately. In a tug of war, both pull simultaneously until one dominates or until the organization breaks.

I want wealth and power

Enjoy what you have

Asura

Deva

When Sandeep's factory was facing high attrition and severe market pressures, he ensured that old loyalists were put in senior positions. They were not particularly skilled at work. They were, in fact, yes-men and not go-getters, who yearned for stability. By placing them in senior positions, Sandeep made sure a sense of stability spread across the organization in volatile times. They were his devas who anchored the ship in rough seas. When things stabilized and the market started looking up, Sandeep hired ambitious and hungry people. These were asuras, wanting more and more. They were transactional and ambitious and full of drive and energy. Now the old managers hate the new managers and block them at every turn. Sandeep is upset. He wants the old guard to change, or get out of the way, but they will not change and refuse to budge. Sandeep is feeling exasperated and frustrated. He needs to appreciate the difference between devas and asuras. Each one has a value at different times. They cannot combine well on the same team but are very good as force and counterforce during different phases of the organization. Sandeep must not expect either to change. All he needs to do is place them in positions where they can deliver their best.

*Devdutt Pattanaik*

# If hindsight is the force,
# then foresight is the counterforce

Brihaspati is the guru of the cautious and insecure stability-seeking devas. Bhrigu-Shukra is the guru of the ambitious and focused, growth-seeking asuras. Sadly, neither do the devas listen to Brihaspti nor do the asuras listen to Shukra.

Watching Indra immersed in the pleasures of Swarga, Brihaspati cautioned him about an imminent attack by the asuras. "They always regroup and attack with renewed vigour. This has happened before, it will happen again. You must be ready," said Brihaspati. Indra only chuckled, ignored his guru and continued to enjoy himself, drinking sura, watching the apsaras dance and listening to the gandharvas' music. This angered Brihaspati, who walked away in disgust. Shortly thereafter, Indra learned that the asuras had attacked Amravati, but he was too drunk to push them away.

After Bali, the asura-king, had driven Indra out of Swarga, and declared himself master of sky, the earth and the nether regions, he distributed gifts freely, offering those who visited him anything they desired. Vaman, a young boy of short stature, asked for three paces of land. Shukra foresaw that Vaman was no ordinary boy, but Vishnu incarnate and this simple request for three paces of land was a trick. He begged Bali not to give the land to the boy, but Bali sneered; he felt his guru was being paranoid. As part of the ritual to grant the land, Bali had to pour water through the spout of a pot. Shukra reduced himself in size, entered the pot and blocked the spout, determined to save his king. When the water did not pour out, Vaman offered to dislodge the blockage in the spout with a blade of grass. This blade of grass transformed into a spear and pierced Shukra's eyes. He jumped out of the pot yelling in agony. The spout was cleared for the water to pour out and Vaman got his three paces of land. As soon as he was granted his request, Vaman turned into a giant: with two steps, he claimed Bali's entire kingdom. With the third step, he shoved Bali to the subterranean regions, where the asura belonged.

Brihaspati stands for hindsight and Shukra stands for foresight. Brihaspati is associated with the planet Jupiter, known in astrology for enhancing rationality, while Shukra is associated with the planet Venus, known for enhancing intuition. Brihaspati has two eyes and so, is very balanced. Shukra is one-eyed and so, rather imbalanced. Brihaspati is logical, cautious and backward looking while Shukra is spontaneous, bold and forward-thinking. Brihaspati relies on tradition and past history, or case studies. Shukra believes in futuristic creative visualization and scenario planning; his father Bhrigu is associated with the science of forecasting. Brihaspati relies on memory while Shukra prefers imagination. Both are needed for an organization to run smoothly.

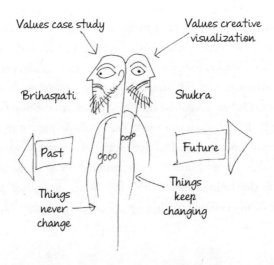

When Rajiv was presenting his vision and business plan to his investors, he realized they were making fun of him. His ideas seemed too strange and bizarre. They said, "Give us proof of your concept." And, "Tell us exactly how much the return on investment will be." Rajiv tried his best to answer these questions, but his idea was radical and had never been attempted before. It was a new product, like the iPad had been at its inception. He would have to create a market for it. He had sensed people's need for it though this need was not explicit. It was a hidden need, waiting to be tapped. Rajiv is a Shukra—he can see what no one else has yet seen. The investors before him are Brihaspati—they trust only what has already been seen.

## Upstream forces need to be balanced by downstream forces

The Purans state that Shiva resides in two places in two forms: he resides on the mountain in Kailas, and down by the riverbank in Kashi. In Kailas he is Adinath, the primal teacher, who offers cosmic wisdom. In Kashi, he is Vishwanath, the worldly god, who offers solutions to daily problems.

Every person is trapped between the god at Kailas who sits upstream and the god at Kashi, who sits downstream. Upstream are the bosses who sit in the central office. Downstream are the employees who face the client. Those upstream are concerned with revenue and profit, while those downstream are concerned with concessions, discounts and holidays. The yajaman needs to balance upstream hunger as well as downstream hunger.

118

We hope that just as we see the devatas upstream and downstream, those around us do the same. When we are not treated as devatas by other yajamans, we too refuse to treat our devatas with affection. Only when we see each other as the source of our tathastu will we genuinely collaborate and connect with each other.

---

At the annual meeting of branch managers, there was much heated discussion. The shareholders were clear that they wanted an improved bottom line. The bank had grown very well in the last three years in terms of revenue, but it was time to ensure profitability as well. However, the customers had gotten used to discounts and were unwilling to go along with the new strict policies that were being rolled out. General Manager Waghmare is in a fix. Kashi wants discounts while Kailas wants profit. Kashi is willing to push the top line but Kailas wants a better bottom line. He is not sure he can make both shareholder and customer happy.

---

# Balance is the key to avoid tug of war

Vishnu has two wives, Shridevi and Bhudevi. Shridevi is the goddess of intangible wealth and Bhudevi, the earth-goddess, is goddess of tangible wealth. In some temples, they are represented as Saraswati and Lakshmi, the former being moksha-patni, offering intellectual pleasures, and the latter being bhoga-patni, offering material pleasures. Shiva also has two wives—Gauri and Ganga—one who sits on his lap and the other who sits on his head; one who is patient as the mountains and the other who is restless as a river. Krishna has two wives, Rukmini and Satyabhama, one who is poor (having eloped from her father's house) and demure, and the other who is rich (having come with her father's blessing and dowry) and demanding. Kartikeya, known as Murugan in South India, has two wives—the celestial Devasena, daughter of the gods, and Valli, the daughter of forest tribals. Ganesha has two wives, Riddhi and Siddhi, one representing wealth and the other representing wisdom. The pattern that emerges is that the two wives represent two opposing ideas balanced by the 'husband'. Amusing stories describe how the husbands struggle to make both parties happy.

The Goddess has never been shown with two husbands (patriarchy, perhaps?). However, as Subhadra in Puri, Orissa, she is shown flanked by her two brothers—Krishna, the wily cowherd and Balabhadra, the simple farmer. In Uttaranchal and Himachal, Sheravali, or the tiger-riding goddess, is flanked on one side by Bir Hanuman, who is wise and obedient, and on the other by Batuk Bhairava, who is volatile and ferocious. In Gujarat, the Goddess is flanked by Kala-Bhairo and Gora-Bhairo, the former who is ferocious and smokes narcotic hemp and the latter who is gullible and drinks only milk. In South India, Draupadi Amman, the mother goddess, has two guards, one Hindu foot soldier and the other a Muslim cavalryman; not surprising for a land that expresses tolerance and inclusion in the most unusual ways. Once again, the pattern is one of opposite forces balanced by the sister or mother.

Balance is also crucial to business. The marketing team needs to balance the sales team. The finance team needs to balance the human resources team. The back-ends need to balance front-ends. Marketing ensures demand generation but its success cannot be quantified as its thinking is more abstract and long-term. Sales gives immediate results and is tangible, but cannot guarantee or generate future demand. The finance team focuses on processes, returns on investment and audit trails, or the impersonal facets of the company. The human resource team has to compensate this by bringing back the human touch. Back-end systems can ensure inventory and supply, but it is the front-end that has to ensure sales and service with a smile. A leader has to be the husband, sister and mother who balances the opposing wife, brother and son.

---

Navin started his career as a sales representative in a consumer goods company. He resented the marketing guys who sat in air-conditioned rooms all day poring over quantitative and qualitative market research data. He resented the fact that they were paid more while it was he who got in the revenue. He carries this resentment till date. Now he is the CEO of a retail chain. He spends all his time with his sales team and the guys on the frontline. He is impatient with his marketing team, tells them repeatedly to go and spend time in shops with the customers. As a result, the marketing team has become tactical about today's sales and this quarter's targets. No one in the company is thinking strategically. The CEO is meeting today's numbers and is not prepared for tomorrow's challenges. This does not bode well for the organization as a whole, or for Navin's career, because he has no one thinking ahead. This is what happens when one wife/brother/son gets more value than the opposing but balancing force.

---

# The impact of an organizational decision is different depending on the source

In the scriptures, different beings live in different spheres. At the lowermost level are the humans. Above them are the devas or gods, led by Indra. Above Indra is Brahma and above him is Vishnu. Shiva is above Vishnu and the Goddess is above Shiva. It is said that when Indra blinks a human dies; every time Brahma blinks, an Indra dies; every time a Vishnu blinks, a Brahma dies; every time a Shiva blinks, a Vishnu dies; and every time the Goddess blinks, a Shiva dies. Thus, the notion of time differs at different levels. And the impact of blinking varies depending on who is blinking.

Organizations, too, have a similar hierarchy in place. At the top sits the CEO, below him sit many unit heads under whom are many managers who have many executives under them. Each one's 'blink' has a different impact on the market.

A leader has to realize two things with regard to this blinking. The first is related to the time-impact of his blink: it takes time for his decision to reach the periphery of his organization, that is, the frontline where people engage with the marketplace. This demands patience. The second is the space-impact of the blink: what seems like a simple decision for the leader has to manifest itself multiple times in the rest of the team. In other words, it has to be understood by many Brahmas. The impact of any error is huge. This makes the cost of an error huge. Large organizations are uncomfortable with such impacts. This is why they control the rate of decisions made upstream in the management chain. Unfortunately, this prevents large organizations from being nimble.

Further, in many organizations it is not clear who is the head.

For example, in the Shiva Puran, Kailas is above Vaikuntha whereas in the Vishnu Puran, Vaikuntha is above Kailas. And not everyone agrees that the abode of the Goddess is supreme. And so, people get confused as to who is blinking and who is staring.

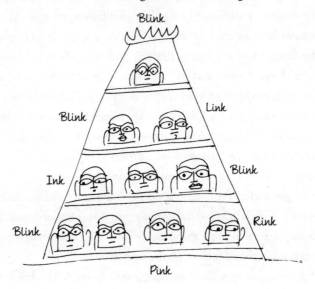

Gyanesh has still not realized the power of blinking. He is currently the head of a 800-strong sales force. Fifteen years ago, he was a salesman renowned for getting things done rapidly. He would take quick decisions and get things done. Owing to this ability, he was very popular in the market and a successful salesman. Fifteen years later, he is still restless and continues to make decisions on the spur of the moment. What he does not realize is that the decisions he makes impact the lives of 800 sales people located across the country. The impact is huge though the time taken for it to show is much longer. By the time everyone in the field understands a decision two months have passed. And by the time they implement the decision, they learn that Gyanesh has changed his mind once again.

*Devdutt Pattanaik*

# In a shifting world, organizations need to be organisms

In the Rig Veda, the organization is described as purush, an outpouring of imagination, an organism. In Jain chronicles, the world is seen as being constantly volatile. It is never stable and is seen as a slithering serpent or sarpa that alternates between an upward boom (sushama) and bust (dushama). Our mind, too, constantly wavers from an optimistic gaze (utasarpini) to a pessimistic gaze (avasarpini), depending on resource availability and market response. With such a view of markets, organizations perforce need to be nimble; they need to be organisms.

The difference between an organization and an organism is that the organization is a thing that is insensitive to the world around it, while an organism is a living being that is aware of the world around it. The organization is a set of rules that people follow whereas the organism is a set of people who follow rules.

Organizations work well when the world around them is stable and predictable. But when the world is unstable, or the market is volatile because of political, economic and regulatory reasons, or because of the changing tastes of the consumer, the organization has to be super-sensitive and adaptable. It needs to be like an organism.

Organizations are of value when one deals with a single market. Organisms are needed when one has to deal with multiple markets. It may be a good time in one market but a bad time in another. In such cases, a global strategy does not help. One needs local strategies. That is why most Indian villages have a local village-god or grama-devata who is linked to the grand, cosmic, distant and abstract bhagavan, who oversees everything. The grama-devata knows how to translate the global view to local conditions. Crisis in a particular village may not affect the whole organization, but it does matter to that particular village. The bhagavan may not give the village as much time and attention as the grama-devata would.

Most villages even have matrix structures in that there is the grama-devata who looks at problems within the context of the village, and the kula-devata who looks at the problem within the context of a particular community that is spread across many villages. Since both the grama-devata and kula-devata are the local communities' manifestations of the global bhagavan, there is enough trust and understanding not to lead to conflict or demands for consensus.

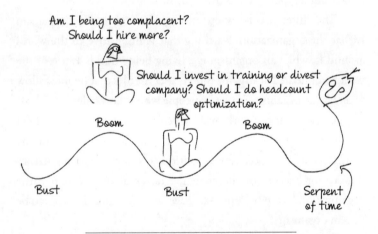

It was a crazy idea but it worked. When Lalwani became the head of the firm, he observed that every department was a silo working in isolation. His leadership team was hardly a team but a bunch of people in the room with no connection to each other. Each of them was focusing on their individual key result area and ignoring the impact on others. So Lalwani came up with an idea. Every six months, the head of a department would make a presentation on the performance of another department and answer questions as if s/he were the head of that department. For instance, Randhir, who headed finance, would make the marketing presentation and Piyush who headed sales would make the human resource presentation. Departments were chosen by lots and to make the exercise serious, it was given a weightage of 20 per cent in the appraisal. Suddenly, everyone was talking to each other. Randhir had to understand marketing, Piyush had to understand human resources. The silos were ruthlessly broken. After much initial discomfort, people started empathizing with each other. The organization became an organism.

---

## In an organism, individual potential and context are taken into consideration

In an organization, the centre takes decisions and those at the periphery follow. In an organism, people downstream (at the periphery) are as sensitive, proactive and responsible as the people upstream (at the centre). For an organization to become an organism, people need to understand both the universal as well as the particular. Everyone needs to see the big picture along with their context specific roles.

Inherent in the word 'leader' is that one who is so decides which direction everyone should go and the rest follow. Yet the leader is located in Kailas, far from the marketplace. His vision is wider, but lacks the local insight that comes from Kashi. Should his garud-drishti take precedence over sarpa-drishti?

To complement the leader's view, everyone else ought to look at the marketplace and then reach a consensus. This is teamwork preventing the autocracy of the leader. However, the people at different rungs of the organizational hierarchy do not have the same gaze, motivations, drive, or even the same line of sight. They will see different things. The eagle will end up fighting the snake and neither will win, except the most powerful, the one with the loudest voice, the one most favoured by the shareholder.

In an organism, every yajaman looks at the devata, and encourages the devata to do the same. Every yajaman clarifies who his immediate team of graha is and who the distant team of tara is. The yajaman works to evoke the potential of his devata and helps him deal with his context so that he delivers. The cascade creates an organism.

To become an organism, an organization has to try to emulate the perfection of the human body. Each of the trillions of body cells that make up our body is sensitive to the big picture as well as the local picture. All of them have the same DNA, but each of them produces only those proteins needed in their location. The eye cell has the same DNA as the skin cell, yet both are structurally and functionally very different, as demanded by their local roles. Every cell is sensitive to the world around itself. Each cell knows that the excessive growth of one at the cost of another is cancer, which will destroy the whole organism, while suboptimal growth is degeneration and death.

Akhilesh's call centre appeared from nowhere and became a major competitor in the industry. What was the reason behind its success? Akhilesh said, "We have strict rules and systems that have to be followed by every manager. But we also have a bypass system that allows the local manager to take quick local decisions without consulting the central business unit head. The centre can in no way predict what will happen in different markets at different points of time. Every client's needs are unique and so we need to have flexible systems, which is rather ironical, as systems are meant to standardize and minimize deviations. The bypass routes make us nimble and also build trust. We do not treat those in the periphery as answerable to the centre; they are answerable to their own balance sheets. For me every employee is a manager and a leader from the first day itself. Only their contexts are small."

# Organisms thrive when the yajaman is flexible

In an organization with Kamas and Yamas, devas and asuras, Brihaspatis and Shukras, garuds and sarpas, Kailas and Kashi, various constellations and planets, there is a need for liminal beings.

Liminal beings are creatures that belong in-between, neither here nor there, but on the threshold. A liminal being is a translator, an intermediary. They enable smooth transactions between different categories, as they are able to see each problem from everyone's point of view and the impact of each decision on various sections of the organization.

Ganesha is one such liminal being. He has the head of an elephant and body of a human, thus he stands at the threshold of the animal and human world. He understands animal fears which ensure survival over millions of years. At the same time, he also understands human imagination that can help us outgrow our fears, take risks, explore unfamiliar realms and create new possibilities.

He can easily move from the role of a manager to the role of a leader.

- As a manager, he has to simplify complex problems. So he yields the axe with the noose.
- As a leader, he has to direct people towards change. So he yields the sugarcane with the elephant goad.

Ganesha's axe is used to slice things apart and his noose to bind loose things together neatly. The axe represents analysis and the noose, synthesis. For the sake of administrative convenience, we can break an organization into departments. But the leader must constantly strive to bind things together so that every part also represents the whole. Unless the parts have knowledge of the whole, every individual yagna of the organizational sattra will not have the right svahas or tathastus.

To direct people towards change, the leader shares the sweetness of his vision and balances it with the sharpness of his determination. A mahout uses the ikshu or sugarcane to draw the elephant in a particular direction. He also uses the ankush or elephant goad to make sure the elephant goes in the desired direction and does not stray from the path. The ankush has two parts attached to the tip of a short iron bar: a sharp tip and a hook. The sharp tip is used to goad the elephant forward. The hook is used to hold him back. The sharp tip pushes and the hook pulls. If the yajaman has to use an ankush repeatedly, it means that his team depends on orders and is not proactive and responsible. It is full of dependent devatas and no dependable yajamans. It means the leader is a karta and everyone else is a karya-karta. Everyone's gaze is towards the leader and not towards the market. In other words, the organization is not yet an organism.

---

Lalit was selected by the head of human resources to serve as the executive assistant to the managing director because he has the ability to understand the managing director's abstract ideas and articulate them in a very concrete, implementable form. Lalit is a liminal being who can easily explain the same problem to different teams in a way that each is able understand. He can easily divide the problem into constituent units and see how each unit can contribute to the whole solution. He is easily able to see the manifold repercussions of a single event. When the company received a legal notice that forced them to recall a product from the market due to trademark issues, he immediately knew how to manage the crisis from a legal, logistical, marketing, sales, financial and people point of view. He knows which branches of the organization to push or pull, coax or threaten. Like Ganesha, he removes all obstacles and ensures the job gets done. And he manages and leads, doing what is appropriate whenever it is needed without throwing his weight around, never once stealing the limelight from the managing director.

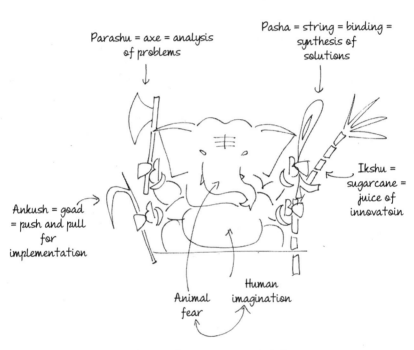

Parashu = axe = analysis of problems

Pasha = string = binding = synthesis of solutions

Ikshu = sugarcane = juice of innovatoin

Ankush = goad = push and pull for implementation

Animal fear

Human imagination

Liminal (moving seamlessly between categories and departments)

# Conclusion

Modern management is all about chasing a target, the Promised Land of Abrahamic mythology, the Elysium of Greek mythology. Hindu mythology, however, warns against chasing Lakshmi, the goddess of wealth; it will result in conflict. Instead they advise making oneself attractive to Lakshmi, worthy of her affection and auspiciousness, so she walks our way. For that we have to be less like Indra, king of the gods, who is consumed by his own hunger, and more like Vishnu, preserver of the world, who is consumed by other people's hunger. Vishnu knows that human hunger is threefold: for wealth, power and knowledge.

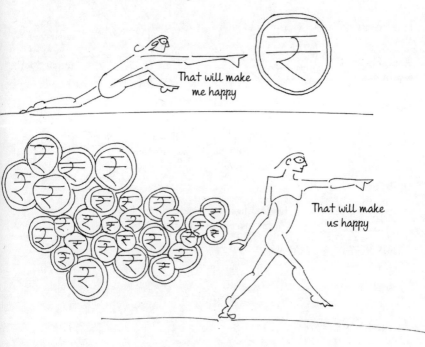

That will make me happy

That will make us happy

As we have seen, at the heart of the Indian approach to management is the ritual of yagna, the oldest of Hindu rituals mentioned in the very first hymn of the Rig Veda. It is commonly mistranslated as sacrifice, or worship, but in fact means exchange, the cornerstone of any economy. When we give in order to get, we are the yajaman. When we give only after getting, we are the devata. When we seek without giving, we are the asura. When we grab, we are the rakshasa. When we hoard, we are the yaksha. When we do not exchange, we are the shramana, or the hermit, who has outgrown his hunger, and so does not seek to be fed, nor feeds. Vishnu is the bhagavan, he who gives despite having outgrown his hunger. He receives only to make the devata feel significant.

The yajaman is a social being: the entrepreneur, the professional, the businessman, the promoter, the manufacturer, the service-provider who satisfies the hunger of a stakeholder, be it customer, employee, vendor, partner, boss or investor, in order to get what he wants. He is always conscious of human hunger, which if not catered to can plunge the world into violence, as we see all around us today.

Modern management has been today reduced to looking at business as a set of targets, or as a set of tasks. But business is essentially about a set of people who satisfy the hunger of the shareholder at one end and consumers at the other. Every stakeholder in business, employees and entrepreneur included, are essentially animals who can imagine. Like every hungry predator, s/he suffers from the fear of death by starvation, hence seeks food. Like every hunted prey, s/he suffers from the fear of death by predation, and hence seeks security and power. This is further fuelled by the imagination, hence creating the insatiable

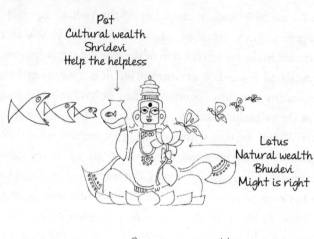

Pot
Cultural wealth
Shridevi
Help the helpless

Lotus
Natural wealth
Bhudevi
Might is right

Animal instinct to dominate, be territorial and aggressive.

Tools that domesticate nature

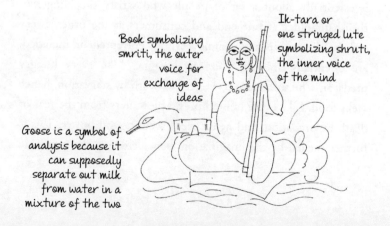

Book symbolizing smriti, the outer voice for exchange of ideas

Ik-tara or one stringed lute symbolizing shruti, the inner voice of the mind

Goose is a symbol of analysis because it can supposedly separate out milk from water in a mixture of the two

yearning for wealth and power in humans. Further, humans wonder who they are, why they exist, and whether their lives have meaning. This fear of invalidation consumes us. Hence, every yajaman needs to have an intimate knowledge of Lakshmi, Durga and Saraswati, the goddesses of wealth, power and knowledge, the hunger for whom exists in different proportions in different stakeholders.

Together the three goddesses (LDS, or LSD, in short) constitute the three arms of human happiness. To make the world a happy place *should be* the ultimate aim of every yagna, hence every business. For this businesses have to be approached as yagnas where we satisfy the other's hunger in order to satisfy ours. That is dharma.

# Notes

With new words are created new worlds, as they are vehicles of new ideas. They enable the process of expanding the mind. The words and terms explained below are common to the books in my sutra series—*Business Sutra*, *The Success Sutra*, *The Leadership Sutra* and *The Talent Sutra*.

|  | Business context | Conventional context |
|---|---|---|
| **agni** | that which is used to tame and control nature | fire god |
| **Amravati** | the ideal goal where all needs are met without effort | Indra's paradise |
| **ankush** | a tool used for pushing people to do their job, and pulling them back | elephant goad |
| **Arjun** | one who argues too much, shooting counter questions like arrows when questioned | the third Pandav who is a skilled archer |
| **asura** | one who feels his entitlement has been denied, resulting in rage and ambition | eternal enemies of the devas |
| **avasarpini** | pessimistic gaze | waning period of an era |
| **avatar** | role adapted to the context for the benefit of the Other | descent of Vishnu |
| **bali** | what is destroyed in the process of creation | sacrifice |
| **bhagavan** | a being who is not hungry but pays attention to others' hunger | a being who is never hungry but feeds others |

| | Business context | Conventional context |
|---|---|---|
| **bhaya** | insecurities | fear |
| **Bhim** | One who wants to act rather than think | the second Pandav who is very strong |
| **bhog** | that which satisfies hunger | consumption |
| **Bhoj** | a leader who balances creativity with accountability | a legendary king |
| **Brahma** | subject of the subjective truth | the creator |
| **brahmanda** | imagined reality | subjective world |
| **chakravarti** | the king who controls his kingdom with rules | emperor of the world |
| **Chandra** | one who is very moody and has favourites | the moon god |
| **Chaturbhuj** | the one who multitasks | another name for Vishnu indicating he has four arms |
| **Chintamani** | that which satisfies every wish | wish-fulfilling jewel of paradise |
| **Daksha** | one who is obsessed with rules | the patron of the yagna |
| **darshan** | observing the subject of subjective reality | gaze |
| **deva** | he who sees what comes to him as entitlement | Brahma's sons who live in luxury above the sky |
| **devata** | he who responds to the transaction initiated by the yajaman | the deity being invoked |
| **Draupadi** | one who has to deal with multiple bosses and subordinates | the common wife of the five Pandavs |
| **drishti** | observing objective reality | vision |
| **Durga** | power that grants security and authority | goddess of war |
| **dushama** | bust | negative period |

| | Business context | Conventional context |
|---|---|---|
| **Ganesha** | one who can easily wear many hats and so communicate between many departments | the elephant-headed god who removes obstacles |
| **Gangu-teli** | the one doing a monotonous job | legendary oil presser |
| **garud-drishti** | strategy, wide vision, long-term thinking | bird's-eye view |
| **Gauri** | organization based on rules | the domesticated form of the Goddess Kali |
| **Goloka** | sustainable happy business | paradise of cows |
| **Gobar-ka-Ganesh** | he who does what he is told to do with no view of his own | legendary dumb character |
| **grama-devata** | the manager who adapts principles of the centre to the realities of the periphery | village god |
| **Halahal** | the negative output of any action | poison that comes with nectar |
| **Hanuman** | he who obeys unconditionally and without question | the monkey who serves Ram and is worshipped in his own right |
| **Indra** | he who wants high return on investment always | king of devas |
| **ishta-devata** | one who grants us personal favours | personal god |
| **Kailas** | where there is no hunger | abode of Shiva |
| **Kali** | marketplace with no regulatory control | the wild form of the Goddess Gauri |
| **Kalpataru** | that which satisfies every wish | wish-fulfilling tree |
| **Kama** | right-brain activity, creativity, which does not like structure | god of desire |

| | Business context | Conventional context |
|---|---|---|
| **Kamadhenu** | that which satisfies every wish | wish-fulfilling cow |
| **karma** | consequences of actions | the cycle of cause and consequence |
| **karta** | the one who gives the directive | a leader |
| **karya-karta** | the one who follows the directive | a follower |
| **Kauravs** | those who stubbornly refuse to learn | the hundred brothers led by Duryodhan who oppose the five Pandavs |
| **Krishna** | he who breaks rules to help others grow on their terms | cowherd avatar of Vishnu |
| **Kubera** | the one who hoards | king of yakshas |
| **kula-devata** | one who grants us departmental favours | the family god |
| **Lakshmi** | wealth | goddess of wealth |
| **Mitti-ka-Madhav** | he who does what he is told to do with no view of his own | folk character |
| **Nakul** | one who looks pretty but delivers nothing | the fourth Pandav who is very handsome |
| **Narad** | he who makes people insecure by comparing and contrasting | trouble-making sage |
| **Narayan** | human potential | God |
| **Narayani** | resources | Goddess |
| **nirguna** | not measurable | intangible |
| **Pandavs** | students who have made mistakes but are open to learning | the five protagonists of the epic Mahabharat |
| **parashu** | analysis | axe |

*Devdutt Pattanaik*

| | Business context | Conventional context |
|---|---|---|
| Parashuram | leader who punishes rule-breakers sternly | the warrior-sage form of Vishnu |
| pasha | synthesis | string |
| prakriti | material world | nature |
| pralay | end of an organization or a market | the end of the world when everything dissolves into the sea |
| purush | imagination | humanity |
| Radha | leader who lets talent go without begrudging them | the milkmaid who is the beloved of Krishna |
| rakshasa | one who takes things by force | demon who grabs |
| Ram | he who follows the rules at any cost to help others grow on their terms | the royal form of Vishnu |
| rana-bhoomi | competitive environment | warzone |
| ranga-boomi | joyful environment where everybody grows | playground |
| Ravan | he who breaks the rule for his growth at the cost of others | king of rakshasas |
| rishi | one who has more insight than others | seer who can see what others do not see |
| saguna | measurable | tangible |
| Sahadev | one who only speaks when spoken to even though he knows solutions to problems | the youngest Pandav who was very wise and never spoke unless spoken to |
| sanskriti | culture | society |
| Saraswati | human imagination | goddess of knowledge |
| sarpa-drishti | tactic, narrow-vision, short-term thinking | snake vision |
| sattra | an organization with many processes | a complex set of multiple yagnas |

| | Business context | Conventional context |
|---|---|---|
| **Shakti** | inborn strength, capacity and capability | goddess of power |
| **Shankar** | he who is content and sensitive to others | another name of Shiva |
| **Sharda** | knowledge of purusha | goddess of wisdom |
| **Shekchilli** | dreamer with no accountability | folk character who dreams |
| **Shiva** | he who is independent but withdrawn from the world | God who destroys |
| **shruti** | personal ideas that cannot be shared | inner voice that is heard but cannot be spoken or transmitted |
| **smriti** | public ideas that are exchanged | outer voice that is spoken or transmitted but not necessarily heard |
| **sthula-sharira** | how we appear physically to others | the physical body |
| **Surya** | one who is radiant and attracts all attention | the sun god |
| **sushama** | boom | positive period |
| **svaha** | input | this of me I offer |
| **Swarga** | Indra's paradise | another name for Amravati |
| **tapasya** | introspection, contemplation, analysis | the practice of churning tapa (mental fire) |
| **tathastu** | output | so be it |
| **utasarpini** | optimistic gaze | upwards movement of time |
| **Vaikuntha** | workplace where everything comes together without conflict | Vishnu's abode in the middle of the ocean of milk |
| **Vaman** | he who grows big and thus makes the Other feel small and insignificant | dwarf avatar of Vishnu |
| **vasudev** | one who is action driven | the hero who is a man of action who seeks wealth |

| | Business context | Conventional context |
|---|---|---|
| **vetal** | facilitator who asks questions that provoke thought, but does not know the answer | the teacher who never goes to the student and who provokes discomforting reflections |
| **Vikramaditya** | the student who goes to the teacher | a legendary king |
| **Vishnu** | he who grows on his terms by enabling others to grow on their terms at their pace | God who preserves |
| **yagna** | the process of exchange | Vedic fire ritual |
| **yajaman** | the one who initiates the offer of exchange | patron |
| **yaksha** | one who hoards | Brahma's son who hoards |
| **Yama** | left-brain activity that is highly structured | god of death |
| **yoga** | outgrowing hunger | alignment |
| **Yudhishtir** | upright but naïve leader | the eldest Pandav |

# Index of Sutras

# ALSO BY DEVDUTT PATTANAIK

## BUSINESS SUTRA:
### A Very Indian Approach to Management

In this landmark book, bestselling author, leadership coach and mythologist Devdutt Pattanaik shows how, despite its veneer of objectivity, modern management is rooted in Western beliefs and obsessed with accomplishing rigid objectives and increasing shareholder value. By contrast, the Indian way of doing business—as apparent in Indian mythology, but no longer seen in practice—accommodates subjectivity and diversity, and offers an inclusive, more empathetic way of achieving success. Great value is placed on darshan, that is, on how we see the world and our relationship with Lakshmi, the goddess of wealth.

*Business Sutra* uses stories, symbols and rituals drawn from Hindu, Jain and Buddhist mythology to understand a wide variety of business situations that range from running a successful tea stall to nurturing talent in a large multinational corporation. At the heart of the book is a compelling premise: if we believe that wealth needs to be chased, the workplace becomes a rana-bhoomi—a battleground of investors, regulators, employers, employees, vendors, competitors and customers; if we believe that wealth needs to be attracted, the workplace becomes a ranga-bhoomi—a playground where everyone is happy.

Brilliantly argued, original and thoroughly accessible, *Business Sutra* presents a radical and nuanced approach to management, business and leadership in a diverse, fast-changing, and increasingly polarized world.

# THE LEADERSHIP SUTRA:
## An Indian Approach to Power
### (Forthcoming: April 2016)

Durga is the goddess of power in Hinduism, as well as in Buddhism and Jainism. Her name is derived from the word, 'fortress', (*durg*). She is the goddess of kings. She rides a lion, the king of the jungle and a symbol of royalty everywhere from China to England. We tend to tiptoe around the role of power in management, and fail to openly acknowledge how the animal desire to dominate often destroys the best of organizations. Critics tend to see power as a negative thing. But power is a critical tool that affects the implementation of any idea. Any attempt to restrain it with rules results in domestication and resentment, and fails to energize the organization. Leaders often equate themselves with lions, and indulge their desire to dominate, when in fact the point of leadership is to be secure enough to outgrow the lion within us, and enable and empower those around us. But this is not easy as anxiety overpowers the best of leaders.

Derived from Devdutt Pattanaik's influential bestseller *Business Sutra*, this book offers startling and original insights into the exercise of power and leadership. It explores the human quest for significance, the power of rules to rob people of self-esteem, and the need for stability even at the cost of freedom.

# THE TALENT SUTRA:
## An Indian Approach to Learning
(Forthcoming: November 2016)

Saraswati is the goddess of knowledge in Hinduism, as well as in Buddhism and Jainism. Her name is derived from the fluidity (*saras*) of the imagination. Human imagination enables us to invent and innovate, visualize, plan and de-risk. Yet imagination is a bad word in the world of business and management. It strips us of certainty. We want to control the imagination of those who work for us, prevent their minds from wandering from work. Yet, every human being lives in an imagined reality. Recognizing this enables us to work with talent, build strong relationships and nurture people to face any situation with faith and patience. Failure to recognize imagination is why family-owned businesses are unable to manage professionals and how professionally run companies end up creating ineffective, mechanistic talent management systems. Training, learning and development, are not just about skills and knowledge and competencies, they are about appreciating the human-animal, recognizing that neither we nor those around us are programmable machines that we can plug and play. Managing people, hence relationships, is key to the survival of an organization.

Derived from Devdutt Pattanaik's influential bestseller *Business Sutra*, this book explores concepts like creativity in the workplace, nurturing talent, and the importance of teamwork. It will help employers and managers become more inclusive leaders who are able to carry their team along with them.